As soon as I fell

A MEMOIR

Kay
Bruner

Gratitude

Self-publishing, at least in my case, is a complete misnomer. I did not do this by myself, and I'm incredibly grateful to friends who were willing to invest their time and expertise in this project.

Alan and E'Lynne Elliot, Pam Gentry, Patty McGeever, and Annie Snyder read various drafts of this book and encouraged me to keep working. Kate King read every draft, and kept asking for more.

I always knew my friend Katrina Ryder was a smart girl, but I had no idea what an extraordinary editor she is, until she got ahold of my rough drafts and unroughed them. I am in awe.

When it came time for the cover, I was without a clue. My friend Christie at Christie Kim Creative made something beautiful out of the confusion.

Andy Bruner, love of my life, leaped over technology with a single bound and kept asking me when the book was going to be done. More than anything, he has loved me until I could finally get these words out into the light.

Special thanks to my children, Libby, Matt, Michael, and Jacob, who seem to have survived what we dished out, relatively intact. They know we'll pay the therapy bills. I love you guys with all my heart.

Contents

Prologue

If I had to pick a moment that makes the story all hang together, it's this one.

There I am, on a Sunday morning, standing in the middle of a gravel road, on a hill in the highlands of Papua New Guinea.

If that moment were a painting, it would be entitled, *Done*.

And if that painting were hung in a gallery, people would look at it and wonder why anyone would choose to paint something as mundane as a 30-something missionary lady, standing in the middle of a gravel road, on a hill, in the highlands of Papua New Guinea.

But as the subject of that painting, I would tell you that it was a watershed moment. The Continental Divide of my life. Everything before went one way, and everything after went another.

It's funny. I remember so very little about that morning.

I don't remember what I fixed for breakfast. I don't remember if the kids had trouble finding clean Sunday clothes. I don't remember what Andy said or didn't say to me.

I just remember leaving the house, walking down toward the meeting house for church. I remember the high curve of the hill on my left, the gravel under my feet, and Karen's front door, down to my right.

I remember what I said. Out of nowhere. The only words I had.

I said, "I can't do this anymore."

Then I stopped in the middle of the road and stood there. Done.

While I was standing there, *done*, Karen came out of her front door and said, "Are you okay?"

I said, "No."

After that, I remember that Karen walked me back home and called Patty, the counselor. There was medication, a little blue pill that wiped my mind clean and shut my body down. Then there was sleep, filled with nightmares.

I thought about dying. In fact, it seemed to me that these thoughts about dying were coming from this one particular corner of the room, right above the doorway.

I was *done*.

Before the moment of *done*, I kept on trying. After the moment of *done*, I was just *done*. That was all I knew: I had tried so hard, and somehow I was *done*.

My husband and I had felt called to the mission field when we were first married. We went to the Solomon Islands in 1993 to work on a New Testament translation for the Arosi language. We had worked hard for 10 years, raising four children and getting the translation done in good time. We were almost finished with the project, just getting ready for typesetting.

We had accomplished everything we'd planned to do, everything we thought God wanted us to do. But somehow, now, I just could not understand my life any more.

This question ran through my mind, over and over: how had trying so hard to do what I thought God wanted me to do, ended up in being so *done*?

Part 1

Where being done began

Childhood

"Saturday's child works hard for a living." — *Traditional*

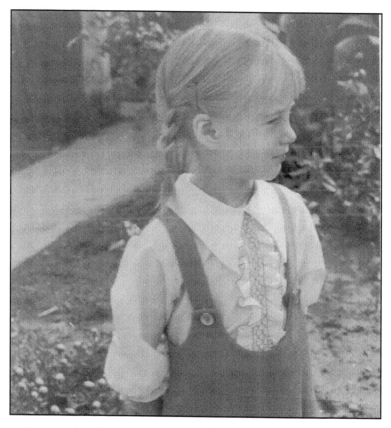

Trying hard was something I'd been doing as long as I could remember.

My parents were missionaries, and I grew up overseas. Mexico, Brazil, Nigeria. I had lived in all those places by the time I was 10. Then my parents moved to Kentucky and settled near my grandparents, my dad's parents.

When I was 10, when we moved to Kentucky, I lost everything I knew, everything familiar. I was used to red dirt and thorn trees and giant termite mounds and thatched mud houses. Leeches in the creek out back. A huge stone on the hill above our house that became my special throne. Spicy bean cakes my dad would buy in town as a dinner treat. Families we knew, with adults, all of whom I called "aunt" and "uncle" and their kids, who I played with every day. With one plane flight, all of that was gone.

Suddenly, there I was in Kentucky, a place where everyone supposedly spoke English, only I found that I could barely understand the accent. At school, all my clothes were wrong. I didn't know the games people played on the playground. During recess I would stand, pressed up against the red brick wall, as close to the door as possible, until it was over and I could go back inside. Some girls asked me to play with them, but I said I felt sick.

Money was tight, so we lived with my grandparents for a while. First in their house, and then in a little apartment built into the barn out back. We had very little, but both of my parents had grown up in farm families. They knew how to make something out of little more than dirt and hard work, and within a couple of years my dad had found some property and built a house for us on a wooded hilltop.

My dad was a fixit genius for all things electronic and mechanical. When we were overseas, he had repaired radios, typewriters, tape recorders, and motorcycles. Back in Kentucky, he worked construction and remodeling jobs, eventually starting his own commercial roofing business.

My mom was a nurse with the local health department, and an expert gardener. She canned beans and froze corn and cooked on a wood stove, up until just a few years ago. She also had seven kids keeping her busy. I was their first child. After me, they had four boys. Then, when I was in high school, my two little sisters were born. My mom rarely sat down, but when she did, she had something in her hands to work on. She was always knitting, crocheting, or mending something.

I never saw my parents disagree with each other. They believed strongly that the husband's role was leadership, and the wife's role was submission. I remember my mom telling me how happy their marriage was, as a result of this system.

My dad had a lot of opinions, and he expressed those opinions with a lot of emotion. Whether it was politics or theology or the rules of the house, it was okay for my dad to be angry, because he was the leader, he was right, and it was his job to make these things clear to us. It was scary for me when my dad was angry and loud, so I did my best to keep him happy by understanding the rules and following them the best way I could.

My parents had been taught that to spare the rod was to spoil the child, and they were very determined not to spoil me. My impression from early childhood is that I was spanked every day. Whether this is true, I do not know. However, I do know that I was spanked with a belt or a spoon countless times. In later years, my mom told me that they had punished me too much. They punished me for things that were just normal childish things. Maya Angelou says that when you know better, you should do better. My parents knew better over the years, and they began to do better as my younger siblings grew up. However, this realization on their part came a little late for me, as all the punishment taught me some erroneous lessons about life and how to make it work.

I came to believe this. Good people didn't have to be punished, because they were good. Bad people got punished, because they were bad. I got punished; therefore, I was bad. I was, indisputably, *a bad person*. I knew this with absolute certainty, from the time I was tiny. Additionally, when we moved to America, I was also different from everyone at school. So I was a bad person, and I was also *a weird person*. On top of this, every couple of years, there was a new baby at home, getting all the time and positive attention that I wished could be mine. All of these circumstances collided in my heart and mind, producing the deep and abiding belief that I was a bad person, strange, strong-willed, stubborn, and unlikable, not someone you'd want to spend time with. I knew there was something inherently wrong with me, and also that it was my job to fix it.

And then, in the mission culture that we were a part of, there was a strong sense of purpose and pride in doing this great work that produced incredible spiritual meaning. If you were unhappy, if things weren't going your way, well, you certainly shouldn't complain. Life was meant to be sacrificial. Lots of people had given up lots of things and were doing great works for God. If you were unhappy, you had a problem. I was unhappy a lot, so clearly I had a problem I needed to fix.

I remember looking through Elisabeth Elliot's book, *Through Gates of Splendor*, as a very young child. It's the story of her husband's death at the hands of Auca Indians, with whom he was working to share the gospel. I was in second or third grade, and I remember sitting in our living room in Nigeria, looking at these pictures of missionaries floating in a river with spears sticking out of their backs, and hearing how heroic they had been. Hearing how, eventually, the Auca Indians had come to Christ as a result of their sacrifice.

Around the same time, a missionary plane went down in our area. We attended the pilot's memorial service, and I have a very clear recollection of walking toward our car afterward, and my dad saying how strong the wife was, how she hadn't shed a tear.

I think those things stuck with me because they were "aha" moments. I was trying to understand how life worked, and I wanted so much to be a good person, instead of *the bad person* I believed I was. To me, these stories provided clues about the kind of life that would make me finally and absolutely into a good person who was worthy of love.

Good people work hard, like my parents did. Good people make sacrifices, like missionaries did. Good people don't worry about their emotions, because they are working so hard and sacrificing so much. They have the joy of the Lord, which is better than happiness. Good people don't need other people, because they look to God for all their needs.

Consequently, I tried to be as perfect as possible. When I couldn't be perfect, my second choice was to perform well. Make it look good. Put on a good show. If I couldn't be perfect, I would look perfect. At least that way, I would avoid punishment and people would think I was perfect, which had to count for something.

I had acquaintances at school, but I didn't have best friends, and I didn't need them. I didn't go to parties or sleepovers. I was fine by myself. In fact, it was better to be alone, because if anybody got too close, the jig would be up. Perfection required distance. At home, I mostly stayed in my room and read until I graduated from high school.

By that time, I had pretty much conquered good behavior. People would comment on my strength, competence, and maturity. I thought I was supposed to be those things, I worked hard to be that way, and that performance-based *goodness* had become my identity, to me and everyone else.

Of course I went to a Christian college, the perfect choice. I met another missionary kid there, our sophomore year. Andy was smart and cute. When we went out on dates, we laughed at the same jokes in the movies. It seemed like having four younger brothers was finally paying off for me, because Andy loved that I could laugh at fart jokes. He was much braver than I was, and not much worried about breaking the rules. I was the oldest in my family, so my every action had been carefully scrutinized. Andy, on the other hand, was the youngest of five boys, and he had learned to fly under the radar early on. He kept quiet and did what he wanted to do. I deeply envied that, even as I constantly struggled to follow all the rules I could find. After our second date, I told my roommate that I thought I could marry this guy, and she thought I had lost my mind.

First Love

I had found a person who liked me, and didn't think I was weird. While I was growing up in Brazil and Nigeria and Kentucky, he had been growing up in Nepal and Papua New Guinea and North Carolina. We each understood the other's odd upbringing. Most of all, he wanted to spend time with me. It felt like hardly anyone had ever understood or liked me, much less wanted to spend time with me, so it was pretty exciting when somebody did. We started dating in April, and when we went to our respective homes for the summer, we wrote daily letters to each other, cementing our initial attraction.

Andy sent funny cards and memorized a Shakespeare sonnet to quote for me and drew an intricate castle with himself, as a stick figure, shouting from the tallest spire, "I LOVE YOU." He wrote things to me like this: "Never in my life have I had a friendship with a girl where I've been able to act myself. I always felt stupid when I began to let myself out of my shell. You make me feel so comfortable."

One time when we were upset with each other about something (neither of us remembers what), he wrote and said,

"There are basically two ways we can understand each other's moods, personalities, ups and downs, pet peeves, etc. Either we can figure it out thru the passage of time or we can save time and heartache by talking about it now. Is this a dumb idea? I'm not sure. All I know is that I don't want to do things that get on your nerves. The only way I can find out is if you tell me." Here was an invitation to speak and to be open that I'd never experienced before. When we were together, we talked and talked. When we were apart, we wrote and wrote.

He was working on a pipeline construction crew that summer, and he was notoriously distracted and forgetful, thinking about me. He left his work boots at home, locked his keys in his car numerous times, and drove through a red light with a fully-loaded pipe truck. People who knew him wondered if I had cast some kind of spell over him.

As for me, I fell deeply in love with this sweet, quiet, hard-working boy who listened to me, respected my opinions, and wasn't afraid to say what he thought, too. He didn't want me to be quiet. He liked me being spunky. We knew we were really different from each other, personality-wise, but we liked the differences. He was good with math; I was good with words. He was adventurous; I was a nester. He thought things out; I felt things through. We felt like we complemented each other well. I felt heard and accepted for who I really was; he felt heard and accepted for who he was, and it was pretty amazing stuff.

To cap it all off, he wanted to be a missionary, and not just a teacher or a builder. No, he wanted to be the crème de la crème of missionary-dom: a Bible Translator, going into a people group without any Scripture, and translating the New Testament into their language.

Of the 7,000+ languages in the world, over 3,000 still had no part of the Bible written down, so there was plenty of work to be done, and we wanted to get in on it. Both of us had grown up understanding the importance of Bible translation, so this was a viable career choice for us. In fact, choosing Bible translation meant that we were going into the family business, and there was a lot of positive feedback for that choice.

All we had to say was, "God is calling us," and that was that. The only way we wouldn't end up as missionaries, was if we failed, by getting cut during the membership process or flunking out during grad school or orientation. My mom questioned whether I could make it as a translator's wife because I liked new clothes and shoes too much, but that wasn't going to stop me. If there were problems with me, I would fix them. I had had a lot of practice fixing myself already. I had found this person I loved, who loved me, who was preparing to do this amazing missionary ministry. If I could stay with this person and do this thing, I might finally be an acceptable person.

I recently found a letter that Andy wrote, that first summer we dated, which should have been a point of caution for us in choosing a Bible translation career. He was dreading the return to studying in the fall and he said this: "When I work with the guys, I feel like a different person, a different personality, than when I am at school. Now there's no pressure, no schedules, no papers to put off, no tests...and I feel so relaxed. It's so sweet to spend the day using my hands and letting my mind meditate on life." Little did we know how much the translation project would resemble school, and how little outlet there would be for Andy to use his hands and let his mind meditate on the good things of life.

We were so young. We had some vague ideas about ourselves and who we really were, but the importance of missionary work, and Bible translation in particular, had been so deeply instilled in both of us that we couldn't imagine a meaningful life for ourselves outside of that context. We ignored and minimized a fair bit of reality, in favor of the sentiment expressed in a popular Christian song at the time, using the words of the slain missionary Jim Eliot: "He is no fool who gives what he cannot keep, to gain what he cannot lose." I was no fool. Failure and imperfection weren't an option on my watch. God was calling, and we would succeed.

First Steps

Fourteen months after our first date, when I was 21 and Andy was 22, we were married, in June 1987. We graduated from college the next year, and went straight into our organization's training program for linguistics and translation. We had our first baby, Libby, right after our second anniversary, and on her first birthday, I found out I was pregnant with our second child, Matthew.

We did our training in Dallas, with summers at the University of North Dakota. When our training was finished, we decided to move back to our college town in Tennessee and build connections with our church there. We knew we would need a place to come home to, and Tennessee was going to be our place.

We moved back to Tennessee, and after staying briefly in a truly squalid basement apartment, we were offered an apartment built into a barn on a beautiful mountain-top property in the country. People thought it was strange, living in a barn, but I had done it before, as a kid in Kentucky, and this apartment was really nice. The family who owned it generously let us stay there rent-free, in return for some mowing and help around the property.

Our priority job during this time was building a team of financial supporters who would pay our salary once we went overseas. To make that happen, we spoke at churches and met with people in their homes. Friends held in-home meetings for us, and introduced us to their friends. Slowly, we built up the financial and prayer team we needed, taking trips all over Tennessee, Georgia, North and South Carolina, and even up into the wilds of Pennsylvania and New Jersey. On those long drives, I often read aloud to pass the time. I remember reading James Herriott's stories of life as a country veterinarian, both of us laughing so hard we would sometimes need to pull over to get ourselves together before we could drive on.

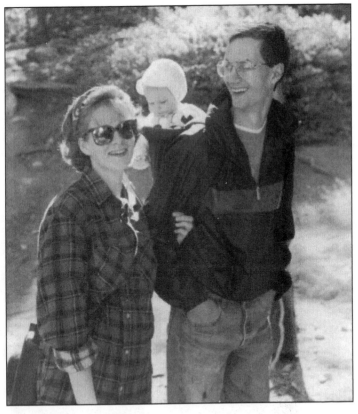

Meanwhile, missionary preparation aside, we still had to pay the bills. We had one car, which Andy used to travel to his construction job, leaving before dawn and arriving home again after dark. He never complained about working so hard. It seemed to me that he could accomplish the work of three people in a day, and he always seemed to be happy doing it. When problems came up, I would feel anxious and upset, but he saw our difficulties as exciting challenges to be conquered. He was so different from me, and I admired the positive way he looked at life and made it work.

While he worked construction, I worked at home and cared for the kids. I loved having my own little nest in the barn, with our daily routines of playing and snacking and napping. I sometimes felt isolated there on the mountain with two babies for company, but I was used to being alone. Also, the isolation seemed like good practice for our future in a small village overseas, and I did love being with the kids. Their little individual personalities just tickled me to death.

Libby was a very outgoing child from the beginning. As a baby, she wanted eye contact constantly. She was 18 months old before she could stay happily in a room where she couldn't see me. When she got older, and we traveled to speak at churches, we would say, "We're going to meet new friends today," and she'd be ready to go. When she was in day care during our training, she was always the most enthusiastic person in the group. One time she was erroneously diagnosed with chicken pox, so she couldn't attend day care. The teacher told me that none of the other kids wanted to do anything without her.

Matthew's personality was very different. While Libby bounced from place to place and gathered friends, Matthew was more cautious. As a baby, he was quiet and almost meditative, like a baby monk. When I'd put him down for a nap, he'd just blink at me, and then happily drift off to sleep by himself. As a toddler, he could be very solemn, and people often told us, "He looks like a little man." He liked to be held and snuggled. If strangers talked to him, he would point at me and say, "Mommy," as if to let them know that he was under my protection. As he got older, he was noticeably compassionate, always thinking about the person who was being left out.

As we prepared to leave the United States, I was concerned about how our missionary life would impact our kids. I knew from my own experience how difficult the transitions could be, and with our backgrounds, Andy and I knew a lot of missionary kids; we had seen the good, the bad, and the ugly. When we were in college, we knew a missionary kid who sat in trees all the time. We knew kids who couldn't make change at McDonald's. We knew people who'd been abused in boarding school. We'd seen a lot of negative things, and I wanted to make our kids' experience as positive as possible. One of our resolutions early on was that if our kids weren't doing well overseas, we would pull the plug and go. Meanwhile, we were going to pay attention and make sure they felt safe and happy, wherever we went. We felt like a good team. Andy could conquer, I could nest, and we'd make it through together.

In February of 1993, we packed up our little family, with our 3 year old daughter and our 18 month old son. We flew to Los Angeles, then boarded the 15-hour flight to Brisbane, Australia at midnight, juggling our sleeping children and our hand luggage. We passed over the International Date Line and from the airplane window, watched our first sunrise over the Pacific. Once in Brisbane, we changed planes for the 4-hour flight to Port Moresby, Papua New Guinea. We arrived in Port Moresby, early in the morning, half-drunk with jet lag and the shock of heat and humidity. We stayed overnight at a missionary guest house before flying on to Madang, Papua New Guinea for 16 weeks of orientation to our new life as Bible translators in the Solomon Islands.

A whole new world

Papua New Guinea, 1993

"I mean to live a simple life, to choose a simple shell I can carry easily—like a hermit crab. But I do not. I find that my frame of life does not foster simplicity." —Anne Morrow Lindbergh

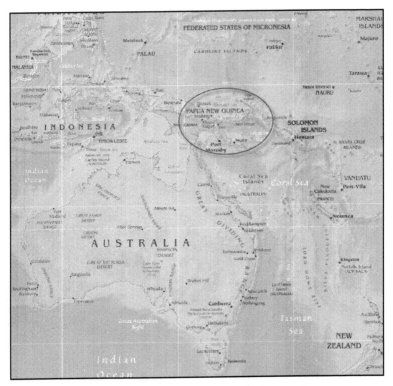

During our orientation, we lived on a mountain-top campus overlooking the South Pacific. We had a 360 degree, billion-dollar view of sunrises and sunsets over a tropical coast. The drive up to the campus, however, was less than

18

idyllic. It was four-wheel-drive accessible only, through a river and then up a single-lane gravel road that hung onto the side of the mountain by the grace of God and the skill of the Papua New Guinean man who drove the road grader up and down on a regular basis.

The first time we made that precarious drive, it had rained heavily the night before, and water came up through the floorboards of the truck as we forded the river. The staffer driving the vehicle took special delight in making the first ride memorable for newbies, I later learned, zipping up the mountain as fast as possible, and straightening every curve he could. I remember hanging onto my kids for dear life, as if somehow I could save them when the truck fell off the side of the mountain and into the jungle below.

Along with a couple dozen other new missionaries, we stayed in a dorm whose paper-thin walls were being slowly consumed by termites and mildew. If anyone's kid cried, we all heard it. If anybody fought, we knew. At the end of the course, there would be a rigorous evaluation of our performance, and there were no secrets. We needed to try hard. As hard as we could.

Thankfully, I was an expert at this.

One of the very first things we learned at orientation was culturally-appropriate conduct for women, so that we didn't offend the nationals around us. In local culture there was a strict division of roles and contact between men and women. Men did men things. They cleared land for gardens, they fished, they hunted, they played pan pipes. Women did women things. They tended the gardens, they cooked, they cared for the children, they swept the yard clean each day. Men talked to men. Women talked to women. In church, the men and boys sat on one side, while the women and girls sat on the other.

I learned that as a woman, I could not look a man in the eye during a conversation. I was required to wear dresses that covered my knees, and the skirt needed to be full and flowing, so that I wouldn't expose my legs. That first day, we learned how to hold our skirts so that we would never accidentally flash anyone while getting up from the floor, where everyone sat. I could not step over anything that a man might afterward handle, because I might contaminate things with my menstrual blood, even if I wasn't currently menstruating. If I went to the produce market, where food would be lying on the ground, I needed to hold my skirt close to my body, because even my skirt floating in the air over the food would contaminate it. I would swim in long shorts down to my knees and I would hike in long skirts down over my calves.

On a surface level, I could go along cheerfully with these cultural norms. It was required, and I was going to succeed. Besides, I was a guest in this culture, so it seemed respectful and appropriate to do what the locals did. Wearing a skirt, wearing a pair of shorts over my bathing suit, these were small sacrifices to make in light of the important task we were called to do. It really shouldn't matter that much.

Deep down, though, these extra rules for women became a subtle reinforcement of the self-condemning framework I already lived in. Every time I had to remind myself not to look someone in the eye, every time I was worried about where my skirt was, or if my shorts were long enough, it whispered in my head that I was not an acceptable person, that there was something inherently offensive about me, and that it was up to me to protect other people from me.

My solution to the shame messages in my head was to not know about them. Most of the time, I hardly noticed. I wore the shorts, I wore the skirts. I kept my eyes down, I kept quiet. One time, I did step over a taro-root at the produce market in

Madang, and it was my most mortifying moment in orientation. I bought the taro, and then threw it away, because of course no one could eat the me-contaminated vegetable at that point.

All of us took classes on local culture, anthropology, and the history of the area. We read books and articles and kept journals of cultural observations. We took classes and practiced conversation in Papua New Guinea Tok Pisin, the local trade language. Tok Pisin is an easy language to learn, we were told. It has a very simple grammar, and a limited vocabulary. Much of the vocabulary is based on English, with some German and local language words thrown in, just to keep it interesting. Within the four-month scope of orientation, we were expected to have a good grasp of Tok Pisin.

For Tok Pisin lessons, Andy and I were placed under the tutelage of a local elder, Papa Kuambi, who had been an evangelist and a pastor in his younger years. After retiring, he moved back to his home village, just down the path from our orientation campus, and became a language teacher and mentor to new missionaries. Papa Kuambi was a tiny person with a huge smile, and he called all of us "my child."

Crazy things would be said in language-learning class on a daily basis. My personal favorite was when one of the students tried to conclude a short story by saying "I am happy" ("mi amamas") but instead said "I am a pineapple" ("mi ananas"). Papa Kuambi had been subjected to years of student foul-ups like this by the time we rolled up, but he was still smiling and listening, looking at our pictures of family at home, and calling us "my child."

We learned how to make a basic shelter out of some branches, plastic string, and a blue tarp. Every weekend, we cooked for ourselves over an open fire in our little shelter, practicing how to survive in a setting with no modern conveniences.

We hiked, because we had to know how to hike. Some of us might end up in places where our feet were the only means of transportation, and some of us had never walked farther than across the parking lot, so we needed to practice. We swam in the ocean, because we needed to know how to swim in the ocean. Some of us were going to end up traveling by boat, and we needed to be able to swim to safety if it came to that. All of us were greatly encouraged to do a one-mile swim by the end of the orientation course, and the one-mile swim presented me with my first serious challenge, physically and emotionally.

When I was a very little girl in Brazil, my family went with a group of other missionaries on a picnic to a river. Somehow, that day, I ended up under water, being swept away downstream by the current. I remember brown water, and I remember not being able to get up to the surface. I remember bumping into somebody's legs, and the owner of the legs reached down and pulled me up to the surface and safety. I learned to swim after that, but I had never since been excited about having my face underwater. Therefore, I was very anxious about the one-mile swim, especially since we'd be swimming in deep salt water with who-knew-what swimming down below. On swim days, I would swim out a little way, panic, and swim back in again. I felt embarrassed that I wasn't doing well enough, and after each swimming day, I thought about going home, back to Tennessee. On the very last swim day, I finally accomplished the one-mile swim, very slowly, with lots of side-stroking that kept my face out of the water. One of the staffers swam with me the whole way, keeping me from panicking. I was happy that I had done the mile swim, but I still felt like I hadn't done it well enough. I was slow. I needed help the whole time. I was pretty sure I would not be able to save myself or anybody else if there happened to be a real water emergency.

Because of my aversion to putting my face underwater, I was hesitant about snorkeling, to say the least. The staff encouraged all of us to try, though, because we were swimming over some of the most beautiful, unspoiled reefs on earth. Eventually, I plucked up enough courage to put on the mask and breathe through the little tube, and fell instantly in love with the colorful coral and fabulous tropical fish that were right below the surface of the water. As long as I was in clear, shallow water, I was happy, just floating, and looking at the pretty things.

Libby and Matt, drinking tree-fresh coconut water, at Orientation

While Andy and I were in class, Libby and Matt and the other kids were looked after by local ladies who came daily from the nearby villages to babysit. The daycare rooms were right in the dormitory enclosure, so the kids played in the courtyard outside our rooms and napped in their own beds every afternoon. The kids seemed to do pretty well in their new environment, largely because the local ladies who ran the daycare program were expert caregivers who genuinely enjoyed the children.

The ladies did more than just babysit. They spoke to the kids in Tok Pisin, so that they would learn the language. They did little lessons on local foods and animals, trees and flowers. They prayed with the kids and taught them to sing a Tok Pisin blessing over their morning snack every day. The younger kids, including Matthew, learned how to nap in a "bilum," a large string bag that worked like a baby hammock. The ladies would carry each baby around in a bilum until they went to sleep, and then they would hang the bilum from a sturdy hook, outside in the shade, where they could catch a little breeze. From these ladies, Libby and Matt first learned to love and trust members of the local community, which set our kids up for a happy future in village life in the Solomon Islands.

Village Living

The finale of our orientation was a four-week stay in a local village, just us and the local family who had agreed to host us. We were experimenting with what it would be like to actually live in a village long-term, in the absence of running water, electricity, indoor toilets, and local grocery stores. If we screwed up too badly, the orientation staff said, "Oh well." It was only for a month, and these poor people wouldn't be stuck with us forever. However, if we screwed up too badly, we could be sent home as unsuitable. It behooved us not to screw up.

Our assigned village was close to a good paved road, about 45 minutes from the town of Madang, where they had things like hotels, swimming pools, and grocery stores. Since we were practicing for village living and not town living, however, we weren't supposed to go into Madang town more than once or twice. To get to town, we'd have to go out to the main road and hitch hike, a task I was extremely disinclined to undertake with frequency anyway, because of the swamp.

When we left the nice paved road, there was a big swamp to cross on foot before arriving in the village. The swamp rose and fell, depending on current rainfall. The villagers had laid a rudimentary bridge of sawn timber close to the village, and most of the time this was all the path they needed to get out of the village, over the swamp, to the road.

In this particular season, however, there had been a lot of rain and there was still a lot of swamp left between the road and the sawn-timber bridge. Someone had brought in huge dump-truck tires and set them in the swamp to close the gap. When we stopped beside the road and started toward the village, we had to take off our shoes and make giant leaps from tire to tire, trying to not fall into the muck. It probably would have been fun, except we were each carrying one of our children, and I was terrified the kids would be dropped and then drowned in the swamp.

The tires were not so bad when you came from the road, because your feet would be dry, and you'd have some purchase on the tires. The tires were bad, though, when you came from the village side, feet already wet and muddy from the timber shifting around in the mire. Every single time we left the village, either Andy or I would end up on our backsides in the mud. As a result, once we got to the village, we stayed, as much as possible.

We had a waspapa ("watch-father") who provided a house for us. The house was up on stilts, with split palm floors. The walls were woven bamboo, and the roof was sago fronds. The house had two rooms: a bedroom and a small storage room. There was a small verandah, which we used as a living room.

Our waspapa had built a split-rail fence around the house, to prevent people from coming up to the house and watching us. It was like Hollywood had come to town, and he was keeping the paparazzi at bay. While we appreciated the privacy, the real value of the fence was keeping out the village's enormous carnivorous pig. During our stay, the pig ate several kittens and I did actually fear that our sweet little Matthew might be its next morsel, if not for the fence.

Most of each day was spent just trying to survive. With no refrigeration, and only the most basic grocery staples, I had to cook every single meal from scratch. Cooking every single meal meant that a fire had to be made for every single meal. Andy took care of building and tending the fire, while I took care of the food prep and trying to keep Libby and Matt from falling into the fire.

We had no running water at our little house. To wash dishes, we carried water from the nearby spring, and heated it over the fire. For hand-washing, we kept a plastic dishpan with water and a little disinfectant in it. We took splash-baths in the shallow creek, and this is where I learned how to take a bath in a sarong, scrubbing underneath while hoping the sides all held together for modesty's sake.

Then there was laundry, which meant another trip to the creek. Every day, I had a bucket of diapers and second bucket of other laundry. I would rub a piece of hard blue coconut-oil soap into a piece of clothing, scrub it with a brush, rinse, wring, and start on the next piece. We quickly ended up with stains and soot in all our clothes, but I kept trying to keep us relatively clean. One day I was scrubbing at something on my favorite shirt, when one of the other ladies said, "Oh, I can fix that for you." I handed it over, and she poured straight bleach on it. Sure enough, that stain was out of there . . . along with all the color. When we left the village, I gave her the shirt.

We drew drinking water from the spring and boiled it, hoping to avoid gastrointestinal issues. We did fairly well until right at the end, when both Andy and I succumbed to horrible diarrhea. The kids didn't get diarrhea, but they did pick up a skin rash of tiny bumps that then opened and turned into tropical ulcers at the drop of a hat. We spent a lot of time cleaning sores and dosing them with antibiotics while the kids screamed like we were killing them.

Our toilet facilities consisted of a little thatched house out back, so short that it only came up to Andy's shoulder. We crawled in and out of there as infrequently as possible, afraid that the spiders and centipedes were finding it much more inviting than we did.

Papua New Guinea is just a few degrees south of the equator, which means that you get 12 hours of day light and 12 hours of dark, regardless of the season. For light at night, we had a kerosene lamp which provided enough light to read by, but by the time we had cooked and washed and sweated and talked to our neighbors for 12 hours every day, we were ready for 12 hours of darkness. So we would creep under our mosquito nets and sweat the night away, and then we'd get up and do it again the next day.

Practical Problems and Errant Emotions

Within the first week or so, we started bumping into issues that we knew we'd have to resolve for longer village stays. This was actually one of the main points of the whole exercise: figuring out how to deal with ourselves long-term in the village. Many of our issues were practical and easily

resolved. We missed cold water like crazy, so in our future
village home, a refrigerator was a necessity. Starting fires was
time-consuming, scary, and stinky, so if we could have a stove
of some sort, that would be helpful. Also, we discovered that
if we sat on the floor for the next ten years, we would probably
be completely crippled. Our backs hurt all the time during
village living, and we needed real chairs. Then we needed
some fun hobbies to occupy ourselves in the evenings, because
without entertainment of any kind, we were starting to get
bored. And finally, we had to figure out how I was going to
get my hair cut.

Before we left the States, I had long hair, down past my
shoulders. This was the 90's, the era of big hair, so my hair
care routine was lengthy, and involved blow-drying, hot
rolling, curling ironing, and extensive hair spraying. I knew I
couldn't do any of that during orientation. For one thing, I
wouldn't have the luggage space for all my hair
accoutrements, and there wouldn't be compatible electricity,
to say nothing of the time involved. I decided to get a curly
permanent, thinking I could just put gel in my hair, scrunch,
and go. We were staying with Andy's parents for our final
weeks in the States, and Andy's mom recommended her
Hungarian hairdresser to me.

I drove to this lady's in-home salon, and told her what I
wanted, making sure to point out that my hair was thick and
heavy and difficult to perm. She took me very seriously,
winding miniscule portions of hair onto the smallest curling
rods, and leaving the perm solution on for the maximum time
allowed. I went there at 2:00 in the afternoon and left at 8:00
that night. I drove home with the car window rolled down to
combat the overwhelming aroma of perm fumes, and when I
walked in the door, Andy and his parents burst out laughing.
The perm I had envisioned as gentle corkscrew curls had

turned into an enormous frizzy afro that no amount of rinsing or shampooing would eradicate.

Humiliation aside, I still thought the perm might work, until we got to orientation and I couldn't fit a hat over the giant ball of curls. I had fair skin, and in the tropical sun, I desperately needed to wear a hat. One of the ladies on staff ended up giving me a really nice short pixie, which I loved. During village living, however, my hair started to get long and the perm wasn't completely gone yet. Desperate hair times ensued.

We had a pair of scissors and Andy was bored anyway, so one day he started cutting. He meant to just trim, but in trying to get the trim even, he would cut one side and then the other and back to the first side and back to the other side, until I was left with maybe a half inch of hair sticking straight up all over my head. We had brought a tiny hand mirror out to the village with us, but we dropped it and broke it the first week so just a shard was left. Using that tiny piece of mirror, I could tell my hair was short, but I couldn't get the full effect. One day I went in to Madang to the produce market with the other ladies from the village, and one of the orientation staffers happened to be there. She took one look at me and burst out laughing. Never in my life had my hair been so entertaining to so many.

Figuring out how to deal with the practical side of life left us with little time to reflect on how we were coping emotionally. Andy enjoyed village living, reveling in all the problem-solving and hands-on work of daily life. To me, it was like a month of camping, which was not my favorite thing, but I felt like I was in a holding pattern. It was easy for me to think, "Well, I'll have a stove, so it won't be this bad," or, "In the Solomons, I'll really get to know people, so I won't feel as lonely." I just tried to make the best of things and wait for better circumstances to make life better again.

Every once in a while in the village, we would have a Community Event. One of our favorite events was the bread truck. One of the stores in Madang would occasionally, with no rhyme or reason we could discern, send out a truck with fresh bread. Somehow, people would know the truck was coming and they'd stand out by the road and wait for it. A couple of times, we got bread that way, and it was like Christmas.

Me, my haircut, and a village friend at Orientation

Another community event was sago-making. Sago was such a staple food in Papua New Guinea that early Bible translations had Jesus saying, "I am the sago of life." I was really excited to see the sago-making process and taste this food that had such history around it.

The process took several days, because first they had to cut down a giant sago palm, using axes and hand saws. Then they sliced it lengthwise, and using a stone mallet, they pounded the inside of the tree into pulp. Then there was a rinsing and squeezing process, which resulted in a fine silt. The silt was squeezed dry, then bundled up in banana leaves, tied together with vines. The bundles were then cooked over low heat to a fine, dry powder.

When it was done, you could eat the sago powder plain. I tried that, and it was about how you'd expect desiccated tree pulp to be: dry and flavorless. You could also mix the sago powder with coconut cream into a drink. I love coconut, so I thought that recipe had potential to be great. But it turned out to be a coconut shell full of glue and coconut chunks. All in all, sago seemed to me like a whole lot of work for very little food quality.

In the end, I left orientation with mixed emotions. The local people were very kind to us, and I didn't think we had offended anyone too terribly, so that was good. When things like the swamp and the sago would happen, I wasn't quite sure how to deal with those experiences. Mostly I tried to appreciate the good things, and ignore the things I didn't like, in light of the really important thing we were going to do. That strategy seemed to work fairly well. When the slimy things happened, we got a good story out of it for the newsletter, and there were no lasting consequences, so we could always say "happily ever after" and go on. Every once in a while, I would have trouble falling asleep or I'd have nightmares, but those little problems would go away and I'd be fine again. At least, that's what I tried to tell myself.

Another new world

Honiara, Solomon Islands, June 1993

"It is not going to be easy to listen to God's call. Your insecurity, your self-doubt, and your great need for affirmation make you lose trust in your inner voice and run away from yourself." — Henri Nouwen

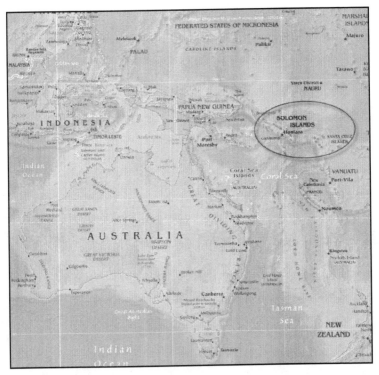

After orientation, in June 1993, we flew one country over, to our final destination, the Solomon Islands. We landed in the capital town of Honiara, on the island of Guadalcanal.

In the Solomon Islands, we joined a group of about a dozen missionary families. The families in our mission group lived and worked in various language projects around the country, and spent time at regular intervals in Honiara. The outer islands had very few Western amenities. If you needed the doctor, the dentist, a new pair of flip flops, or a bag of sugar, you could only find those things in Honiara. If you wanted to call home and hear your mother's voice, the telephone was in Honiara. Hence, visits to Honiara from the outer islands were a necessary part of a language project in the Solomons. Our group owned a few houses that could be rented as needed, along with a number of group vehicles that were available to share.

When we arrived, we planned to spend a few months in Honiara, before relocating to another island in the Solomons for our language project. Once we were established in the language project, we anticipated spending three or four months at a time out in the language area, with regular trips back to Honiara for the supplies and support we knew we would need.

As we flew in, the beauty of the country took my breath away. Hundreds of green islands dotted the South Coral Sea, a million shades of blue. Palm trees leaned out along the shore. Black rocks broke up the sand. Scattered roofs slept in the sun, soft brown thatch or glinting tin. A single road threaded its way along the beach, tracks spidering inland at sporadic intervals.

The airport is centered around a runway built by the Japanese, and occupied by American troops during the battle for Guadalcanal in World War 2. In fact, much of the original infrastructure of the island was constructed during World War 2, by either the Japanese or the Americans.

The road we traveled from the airport into Honiara essentially ran from one battlefield on the eastern end of the island, where American Marines had landed, to another battlefield on the western end of the island, where the Marines finally pushed the Japanese off Guadalcanal. In the battle for this strategic island, so many ships and planes had been sunk in the waters that the harbor in the town of Honiara was known as Iron Bottom Sound.

There were still gun mounts we could visit, and in one place, a road grader had been left to rust in the jungle so long that a tree had grown up around it, gradually lifting the grader up onto its back tires. The hills around Honiara were still covered with foxholes, where objects like bullet casings, uniform buttons, helmets, and war-era Coke bottles could easily be found. There was still a police unit that was routinely called out to deal with the unexploded bombs people would find when digging new gardens. The hospital in Honiara was still casually called by its US military map number: Number 9. The cemetery was referred to, ghoulishly, as Number 10.

When we first arrived in Honiara, the road appeared to have had little maintenance since the Marines had left it there, 50 years before. It was composed of very little tarmac, and very many potholes. Theoretically, everyone was supposed to drive on the left hand side of the road. In reality, everybody just picked the least potholed part of the road and went there. Traffic never moved above 10 miles per hour, but the holes were so deep that even at slow speeds the jolting was absolutely brutal, to say nothing of the noise. Driving in Honiara was like traveling in a tin can full of rocks, if that tin can was sitting in a sauna, at a year-round temperature of 95 degrees with 95 percent humidity.

After the shock of that first bone-jarring journey, it was a relief to arrive at the house we were renting. It was up on a ridge, overlooking the Coral Sea, with islands off on the horizon, flame-colored Poinciana and white frangipani trees blooming in the yard, and an afternoon breeze coming up from the water.

After years of preparation—college, post-graduate linguistics courses, fund raising, frugal living, leaving family, leaving home—finally we had arrived in the Solomon Islands, ready to begin this task we had anticipated for so long.

At this point, Andy was pretty excited about all the new challenges ahead. He had enjoyed the varied tasks of village living and looked forward to more exploring and problem-solving. For me, however, the excitement was seriously tempered by months of temporary living. We had stayed with Andy's parents for several weeks before leaving the States. We had been on the orientation campus for three months. We had done village living. Then we had gone back to campus for a couple weeks of closure. Now we were in Honiara, just another stop on the road to our final home in the village. In six months, we had moved 4 or 5 times. I was ready to nest in a big way, but I would still have to wait for our new village and the idealized missionary life in my head, the life I hoped would be settled and serene again.

Before we started out on this journey, I expected, at this point, to be feeling inspired, and perhaps a tad heroic, since I was now being the ultimate good person. I was still trying to convince myself that I did indeed feel thrilled. Deep down, though, I was scared and trying not to be scared. I was having to pretend, a lot, that I could cope with the realities of daily life.

Reality Bites

The first disturbing reality was how much I hated language learning. I had survived learning *Tok Pisin*, mostly because Papa Kuambi was so encouraging, and so sweet that I couldn't bear to disappoint him. Now, however, I had to switch over to *Solomons Pijin*, supposedly a closely related language. During our first week in-country, I listened to a story in *Solomons Pijin* on the radio. I understood that the subject of the story was a bird. After that, I was clueless. It was a pretty discouraging moment.

The worst part about not understanding *Solomons Pijin* was this: *Solomons Pijin* was just the beginning. We weren't going to stay in Honiara, where people regularly used *Pijin*. We were moving out to a village on another island, where there would be yet a third language to learn: *Arosi*. I was starting to feel like all these languages weren't going to fit in my head.

I was also trying to learn how to cook, so that we could survive. I had cooked during orientation, but that was over a campfire, and campfire cooking was not a long-term solution when it came to keeping body and soul together. After campfire cooking and subsequent jungle intestinal ailments at orientation, Andy, all 6 feet 2 inches of him, weighed about 130 pounds. We needed to eat, and eat well. Immediately.

I assumed that, once I had a regular stove and fridge, and lived in a town, I would be able to feed us pretty well. Surely it was simply a matter of shopping and cooking, both of which I had long ago conquered as an American housewife. Or so I thought. It turned out that shopping and cooking in Honiara was a whole new ballgame, and there were new rules I needed to learn.

First, there was ONE sacrosanct food-buying rule, the rule that ruled them all: *if it's in the store, buy it immediately.* Since everything in the grocery stores came over from Australia and China by ship, the food supply came in waves. When a new shipment arrived, there was plenty to buy. Soon enough, though, supplies would dwindle and we'd be left waiting for cheese and milk powder and whole wheat flour and butter, until then next ship would arrive. Each store had its own varying stock, so we would check each store to see what we could find. When special things like carrots or apples were sighted, whoever found them was honor-bound to call everybody else and share the news, because such delicacies would disappear quickly.

Second, there was the car-sharing rule: *check with your neighbor before taking the van.* We couldn't just jump in the car and go whenever we wanted, because we did not own our own vehicle. Our missionary group owned three or four 7-passenger vans, which we all shared with whoever else happened to be in Honiara at the time. Usually the sharing went smoothly, but occasionally someone would revert to their normal Western frame of reference and rattle off with the van, right when somebody else was expecting to use it, and that would be very bad for community relations. We could not forget the car-sharing rule.

Third, there were traffic rules. There was only one brutal potholed road along the coast, leading into the downtown shopping area. To get to the groceries, we had to drive on that road. The traffic rules resulting from this unpleasantness were these:

1. *Go to town as little as possible.* We didn't just dash into town for a gallon of milk. For one thing, there was no gallon of milk to be had. We mixed up our own milk with milk powder each morning. But mainly, dashing, under our traffic conditions, was simply not possible. Going to town was a major expedition, so we learned to go once a week at most. I had a list of every single kitchen ingredient, along with the amount of that ingredient that we used each week: ¼ cup baking powder; 1 dozen eggs; 3 cups of lentils. We stocked up according to the list, eliminating unnecessary trips to town.

2. *Never turn back.* Due to the number and depth of potholes, everyone else had to drive as slowly as we had to, which made traffic creep along at a pace that made snails look speedy. No jar of peanut butter, no loaf of bread was worth the misery of turning back and going through the whole traffic experience again. Since we drove (theoretically) on the left, we would stop at stores on the left, all the way to the end of town. Then we would swing (slowly) through that magical British traffic invention, the Roundabout, and come back up the road, stopping at any stores we needed on the other side of the street. On a regular shopping day, the routine would go something like this: bakery, peanut butter store, grocery store, post office, roundabout, stationery store, produce market, cross the bridge into China Town, egg store, bulk food store, grocery store, grocery store, home.

By the time each shopping trip ended, I would be completely exhausted by the dust, noise, bone-jarring pot holes, and sweat that passed for normal in our sauna-like environment. What's more, the results of all this hard labor were often disappointing, when the stores did not yield the ingredients I had hoped for.

The first time I was taken to buy groceries, I stood in a shop in China Town called QQQ, and I thought, "We will starve to death." We were at the end of a food cycle, waiting for a shipment, and there was very little on the shelves. Rice. Tuna. Flour. Sugar. Jam. Pickled Beets. Corn. Powdered milk. My assignment: make a palatable meal. Go! It was like some demented reality-TV cooking show that never ended.

While supplies ebbed and flowed at the grocery stores, there was always a large farmer's market which provided us with tropical fruits and vegetables. Tropical bananas were a revelation of shapes and sizes and colors and flavors. The

Chiquita banana we knew in the States did not exist, but its cousins were plentiful and delicious, and ranged in color from light yellow to deep purple. Papaya was another main fruit staple, in season year round. We ate it almost daily, with lime juice and a sprinkle of sugar. We loved the mangoes, which came into season at seemingly random intervals. Around Christmas time, we looked forward to pineapple season, when shiploads of sweet and juicy pineapples would arrive from the province of Malaita.

While we loved the fruit, tropical vegetables were much harder for us to get used to. Our common American staple vegetables: carrots, broccoli, green beans, white potatoes, and salad greens didn't grow in the tropics. The most common local vegetables were endless varieties of leafy greens. I had never cooked a leafy green in my life, and the ones we'd had cooked for us during orientation were some kind of okra relative. When boiled, they turned slimy. Over time, we all came to enjoy greens—especially when cooked with coconut cream. Coconut cream, in fact, was the cure for all leafy vegetable ills. Whatever it was, if I cooked it in coconut cream, it would always be better.

Tropical root crops—yam, taro, purple and yellow potato—grew in abundance. When I tried to treat these like the white potatoes I was used to, though, strange things happened. The yellow potatoes looked enough like white potatoes that I thought they would cooperate in creating mashed potatoes. They would be boiled up normally enough, but as soon as the mashing process began, they would set up like concrete, no matter how much milk and butter I tried adding. I eventually learned that any root vegetable, sliced thin and deep-fried, generally becomes a good French fry. It took me a couple of years to formulate two simple cooking rules: 1. *Put it in coconut cream*, or 2. *Deep fry it*. With all the sweating we did, calories weren't much of a concern. In fact, if Andy gained weight, I was overjoyed.

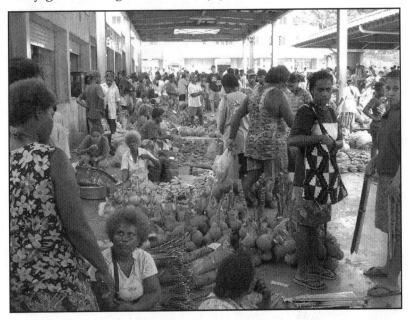

Meanwhile, the shopping occupied long, sweaty hours. The cooking required even more long, sweaty hours. Unfortunately, the results at dinner time seldom reflected the huge effort I had expended, in trying to create a palatable meal. When I did have a successful meal, it was such a momentous occasion that I felt obliged to report back home about it. I didn't realize how much I was writing about food, but Andy's mom told me years later, "I never knew anybody who wrote about food as much as you did." It was hard to explain to people with regular food options how limited our choices were, and therefore how thrilled I felt with my occasional success.

Eating out was a challenge in the Solomons, too. There was no fast food, and no dining with affordable or appealing options to a family with small children. There were one or two "nice" restaurants, catering to the few expatriates who worked in the banking and development sectors. The first time Andy and I went on a date to the nicest restaurant, we saw a rat climb over the dining room wall into the kitchen. One time we took the kids out to a hotel for lunch after church, as a treat. After looking at the menu and making our selections, we told the waitress what we wanted. After we named each item, she said, "Oh, so sorry, that's not available."

Finally, we asked, "Well, what IS available?"

"Fish and chips," she said. We all got fish and chips, which the kids loved.

After a while, we found a Chinese restaurant, upstairs and in the back of a Chinese store, where we became weekly regulars for several years, whenever we were in Honiara. The owners lived just across the hall from the restaurant, and over the years we watched their daughter grow up as we ate our way through countless plates of fried noodles. As a toddler, she threaded a little push-tricycle through the tables. Later on, she got a peddle tricycle. Eventually, she graduated to a two-wheeler with training wheels, which she maneuvered around the restaurant like a circus clown.

Since eating out was more of an adventure than a way to feed ourselves regularly, I learned to make things from scratch that I had no idea you could make from scratch: tortillas, pizza, yogurt, granola. All the time, I found myself substituting one thing for another, with varying results. Picking weevils out of rice, flour, pasta, oats, raisins, and popcorn became normal. In spite of my many hours cooking, things often didn't taste right, because many times the amount of weevil "dust" was equal to the original product. I spent as little time as possible thinking about what that weevil "dust" might actually be, since there was nothing we could do but eat it anyway.

When I looked around me, it seemed like the other missionary women in our group were doing just fine. Of course, most of them had been there for three years or more. Yet, in spite of this knowledge, I wasn't capable of giving myself time for a learning curve. I persisted, trying to be perfect. I felt like I wasn't doing so well, and I was completely intimidated by these women who seemed to do this crazy life with such ease. In my head, in my perfect world, I needed to get it right, immediately.

The first time I walked into the house we were renting from the group, I found forty yards of fabric with meticulously detailed instructions about how to sew curtains for the living room. These instructions seemed like rules to follow, so there I was, obediently sewing in a sauna, with a borrowed sewing machine that gave a vicious shock at random intervals, and forty yards of pink and white tulip-y things on a dark blue background. It was not a fun job, but sewing was something I could competently do, so I sweated hard and got it done.

When the curtains were finished, we had another missionary family over for dinner. The wife walked in, pointed, and said, "That panel is upside down." Sure enough, I hadn't noticed, but the flowers had a right-side-up and an upside-down. Accidentally, I had sewn one panel upside-down. I told her that I would fix it, but I never did. Privately, I kind of enjoyed walking into that house, even many years later, and seeing that nobody else had cared enough to fix that upside-down panel either.

I was bad at language learning. I couldn't shop or cook. I made curtains upside down, and even left them that way. Then I had to be the family doctor, and I was pretty sure I would be bad at that, too, with life-threatening consequences.

Our medical advice amounted to a little brown book on tropical medicine that we studied at orientation—and my interpretation of said book. I had a big Tupperware box full of medicine, and if anybody in our family ran a fever, I treated them with chloroquine for malaria. Or possibly gave them antibiotics for an infection. Well, probably both. Just to be safe. It wasn't just the big scary tropical diseases, either. Any tiny break in our skin—even a prick from a sewing needle—could turn into a major infection if we didn't get antibiotics and a band-aid on it right away. I worried about using so many medications and antibiotics, but one of my friends said that we lived in a cesspool of tropical disease, so something always needed to be killed off. Since we needed so many medications, it was fortunate that we didn't need a prescription to get them. We could simply go into the pharmacy and ask for anything we needed.

Just a few weeks after our arrival, Andy came down with malaria, and had a seizure while sitting on the toilet. Another missionary drove us to the hospital. When the doctor arrived, my medical and language incompetencies collided, as our missionary friend encouraged me to practice my language skills by telling what happened in *Pijin*. I had yet to learn the phrases for toilet and seizure, so I abandoned the attempt pretty quickly. Fortunately, the doctor spoke fluent English and Andy got the medicine he needed. I worried about what would happen when we were in the village, though. I just didn't think I could provide the kind of medical care my family was going to need.

Somebody had sent me a card that said, "The will of God will never lead you, where the grace of God cannot keep you."

I kept hoping this was true, and that somehow on the way to the village, I would morph from my incompetent, frightened self into the superwoman that the job appeared to require.

Yet another new world

Tawatana Village, Solomon Islands, October 1993

"Sail away from safe harbor. Catch the tradewinds in your sails. Explore. Dream. Discover." — Mark Twain

"Also, throw up." — Kay Bruner

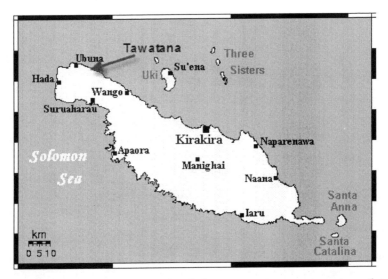

When we arrived in the Solomons, we were assigned to work in the Arosi language, on the island of Makira. After four months in Honiara, adjusting to life in the Solomons, we were finally ready to head out for our first visit to our assigned language group, and the village that we would call home for the duration of our translation project.

The Arosi people, about 7,000 in number, occupy the western quarter of the island of Makira. They live on two distinctive coastlines. The northern coast is on the interior side of the island, facing the other islands in the Solomon

Islands chain, which block the worst of the big ocean waves. The southern coast faces the open ocean, resulting in stormy seas, changeable weather, and its nickname: *The Weather Coast*.

The language is likewise divided into two closely-related dialects, one on either side of the island, inventively called *Arosi One* on the northern coast and *Arosi Two* on the southern coast. Relationships are cordial between the two groups. Groups of women visit back and forth regularly, bringing gifts to one another. The men's pan-piper musical groups of *Arosi One* tour *Arosi Two*. Soccer games for the men and netball tournaments for the women are organized between the two groups for the Christmas holidays.

Social interaction is impeded only by the fact that there is no road for vehicles, so travelers go by motor canoe when the weather allows. Otherwise, moving from one side of the island to the other takes a good day's walk. And once you stop to greet everyone in villages along the way, it might take a couple of days.

The people are subsistence farmers, which means their days are spent gardening to provide enough food for them to live on. They mostly farm root vegetables: taro, cassava, and varieties of yam and sweet potato. These are usually cooked in a delicious soup with leafy greens and coconut milk. They fish on the reef, and gather spiny sea urchins to roast. Everyone loves to supplement local produce with rice and two-minute noodles (like Ramen), shipped in from Honiara, but these cost money, and money is scarce. Most people live out of their gardens and off the reef.

The Arosi people have a 100-year tradition of Christian worship, with both the Church of Melanesia (Anglican) and South Seas Evangelical Church having established churches in the area. In a culture where equality in relationships is paramount, there are no dissenters. The community is Christian, so individuals are Christian. Our job in the community was not to evangelize or to convert people to Christianity. We came to support the local church by helping them to translate the New Testament into their own local language.

The Church of Melanesia was an early proponent of the use of the vernacular in worship. The first Anglican priests created an alphabet, recorded the Arosi language in writing, and translated the Book of Common Prayer. In villages throughout Arosi-land, morning and evening prayers were read in Arosi. An Arosi hymnal had also been created and was used daily. No one had had the time or expertise to tackle the full Bible, however, so readings from the Scripture were still done in English.

Those first English-to-Arosi translations were translated word for word, so literally that they were almost incomprehensible. They often disregarded Arosi grammar, and used meaningless vocabulary. It helped me to understand how meaningless those literal Arosi translations were, when I shopped for toys in Honiara, and read their descriptions, translated literally from Chinese. I found an "Argent Batman:" "the technology have change, than the power is in the tiptop," and "Golden Batman:" "Not only in the night, the power of the sun is in point." The words were English, but there was no meaningful content whatsoever. Without the application of good translation theory and principles, any text translated word for word into the Arosi language was just as meaningless.

Early on, one of the ladies said to me, "The prayer book in Arosi and the Bible readings in English are kind of the same. Some words I understand and a lot of words I don't." The literal Arosi translations were almost incomprehensible and

English translations were equally difficult for local people to understand.

Though English was taught in school throughout the Solomons, after leaving school, most people only heard English in church. Truthfully, their comprehension of English after learning it in school was a lot like my comprehension of German after learning it in school: very limited. Yet, despite these barriers, they were still going to church, morning and evening, attempting to relate to God in languages they couldn't really understand. We could see that there was a huge need for good, understandable translation to be done. If people were going to church, we thought, they should at least understand what they're doing there. We could help with that.

Leaders in the upper echelons of the Church of Melanesia wanted to see their services conducted completely in the vernacular, and invited our organization to participate in Bible translation and literacy projects throughout the country. The idea was that members of our organization would work as advisors to local translators, guiding and training them through the process of translating the New Testament. By the time the New Testament was done, we hoped that there would be enough local expertise to continue on with translation of the Old Testament with less outside help from expatriates like us. The Church of Melanesia had chosen Arosi as the next translation project, so when we arrived, that's where we were assigned.

We were told that we would live at the village of Ubuna, population 500 or so, where the district priest could look after us. There was a small medical clinic at Ubuna, with a nurse in residence, and I was happy to live as close to that nurse as possible. We were told that several villages were organizing themselves to build a house for us, made of local materials:

woven bamboo walls, split palm flooring, and sago leaf roofing. While we were still in Honiara, Andy was able to use a two-way radio to talk to the priest at Ubuna, who sounded happy to host us. He assured Andy that our house was underway and would be ready soon.

Within a few weeks, the Bishop of the island of Makira invited Andy along on his annual tour of the diocese. The Bishop and his entourage would board the church's ship, *Southern Cross*, in Honiara, and then spend two weeks around the island of Makira, visiting each of the parish churches. He would baptize babies, perform weddings, and offer Holy Communion to his parishioners.

Andy was glad to go along, get to know the Bishop, and have a first look at our future home. Another radio conversation with the village priest assured us that the house was almost finished, so we decided that Andy would take out some of the bigger household items in preparation for the whole family's move to Ubuna in October.

While we were prepared to live in a local-style sago-leaf house, we had learned from our experience at orientation that we did want a few comforts. We had a load of supplies for setting up a household, plus consumables for a 3-month stay. Our supplies included: chairs, mattresses and linens; buckets of dried beans, rice, pasta, flour; cases of canned fruit, vegetables, and tuna; drums of kerosene; solar panels and batteries; our computer and two-way radio; books, stationery, office supplies.

We had a tiny refrigerator that held 10 pounds of cheese and 5 pounds of margarine. Five pounds of ground beef would fit in its miniscule freezer, packed into ¼ pound patties, smashed flat. We had a two-burner stove that had been wrested from a camper van. Its one oven shelf exactly fit a 9x13 pan, if the pan didn't have handles. Both the fridge and stove ran off the propane gas that we would transport to the village in silver 100-pound bottles.

The Bishop was happy for Andy to take those things out on the *Southern Cross*, and so, one breezy evening, they sailed off. At Ubuna the next morning, they radioed ashore to let the village priest know that Andy was arriving with the stuff, and they were going to bring it ashore and put it in the new house.

"Well," said the priest. "The house isn't quite ready yet."

"Not quite ready yet?"

"Well, they haven't really started it."

That was our first experience with a cultural phenomenon we would encounter over and over again. In our orientation, we had been told, "This is a relationship culture." It was true that people were very pleasant, accommodating, helpful, and willing to bend over backwards to help us be happy, and that was wonderful. However, we also found that, many times, in the interest of happy feelings and harmonious relationships, people would say things that were not exactly the truth. Like: the house is almost finished. When in fact, it was still growing in the jungle. I was a past expert at saying and doing things to make other people happy with me, but there was a fine line in my head between saying things to make people happy and saying things that they would inevitably discover to be total fiction. Clearly, in Melanesian culture, that fine line was drawn in another location, whose exact longitude and latitude we had yet to determine.

So there was Andy, with all this stuff and no house, and, evidently, no house for the foreseeable future.

One of the other passengers on the *Southern Cross* that day was an older gentleman, called Mr. Ben. He was a school headmaster, nearing retirement. In anticipation of his retirement, he had built a house in his home village, Tawatana, which happened to be just down the coast from

Ubuna. Hearing what was going on, he said to Andy, "I have this house in Tawatana, and it's just sitting there empty. You're welcome to use it, until I need it when I retire next year."

Amazingly, this man gave us his brand-new house, rent-free for a year, the retirement home he had built with the money he had saved throughout his career as a teacher. It boggled our minds that a stranger would do this for us. Having someone show up at just the right time, in just the right place, with a brand-new house, became a real evidence to us that God had put us exactly where he wanted us to be. Our village home, therefore, became Tawatana rather than Ubuna.

Moving to Tawatana

Once Andy returned from his tour with the Bishop, we were ready to get into a routine and start on the language project. Our plan was this: we would go out to Tawatana for a 3 or 4 month stay, return to Honiara for a few weeks to replenish supplies, then go back to the village again. That would be our routine. Everything depended on the local ships' schedules, though, and we quickly learned that these schedules were dicey in the extreme.

Our very first trip to the village demonstrated this unpredictability, when Andy ended up traveling out separately from the kids and me.

Even though Andy had taken the initial load of supplies out to Mr. Ben's house in the village, we still had more stuff. We were moving to a place where we couldn't buy so much as a carton of eggs, and I wanted to build a safe and happy nest for my little family, so we had lots of stuff. Our supplies were loaded onto a cargo ship one afternoon, with a projected time of departure around dark. We planned to travel on this same ship with our supplies. Ships out to our village typically sailed all night and arrived at Tawatana mid-morning the following day. In fine seas, the trip takes 12 to 14 hours. In rough seas, the trip is longer.

Our supplies were loaded onto the ship in the afternoon, and we arrived at the wharf that evening, ready to go. However, we learned that the crew hadn't refueled the ship before the fuel depot closed for the night. Now, we learned, the ship would be refueled and leave sometime the following day, which meant that it would likely arrive at Tawatana in the middle of the night.

Arriving at night was a problem, because there is no wharf at Tawatana. The ship stops at the mouth of a creek, where there's a break in the reef. Then the ship's dinghy is lowered, the cargo hold is opened, and all of the cargo gets tossed up out of the hold, and then down over the side of the ship—8 or 10 feet—into the dinghy. Then the dinghy goes ashore, pulls up on the beach, unloads, and returns for more cargo, and eventually the passengers.

Getting the cargo off the ship in the dark was not optimal, but it wasn't the deal-breaker.

The deal-breaker was getting me and our two toddlers over the side of the ship and down the 8-10 foot drop into the dinghy in the dark. Since Andy had been out to the village with the Bishop, he had experienced the dinghy-drop a few times and he wasn't going to put me and the kids through that in the dark. He was really afraid we would not survive it.

Because here's what happens. The ship rolls back and forth on the waves, while the dinghy bobs up and down. A departing passenger must time her leap just right, when the ship rolls down and the dinghy bobs up, in order to board the dinghy in one piece and relatively dry. I had no confidence in my ability to survive that leap of faith in the dark. More to the point, I certainly wasn't going to toss my 4-year-old and my 2-year-old off the ship and into the dinghy in the pitch dark.

A selection of ships, Honiara, Solomon Islands

Unfortunately, it wasn't possible for the cargo to go on the ship without somebody to make sure it arrived at the proper village. While we didn't think anybody would steal from us, we had to be there to tell the ship's crew where to stop. We were in a quandary, because the supplies were already on the ship, buried in the cargo hold, and the ship and the cargo were going. We decided that our best option was for Andy to go with the cargo, meaning that the kids and I would make our first trip to the village without him. This was far less than ideal, but we didn't know what else to do. The dinghy in darkness with small children was non-negotiable.

Andy got onto the ship, spent the night, and then puttered away toward the village at first light. By happenstance, there was a small passenger ship headed out to Tawatana a day later, so the kids and I planned to travel that way.

Then, it turned out that Andy's ship didn't stop at the right village. In subsequent trips, the ship's captains all figured out where the white family lived, but it took a while, and that first time, they just didn't know. Though they had assured Andy that they would wake him when they got to Tawatana, in the dead of night, they cruised on past. There were no lights in the village, nothing you could see from the ship. The stopping point was merely a break in the reef like so many others, which they failed to identify correctly in the dark.

When they finally stopped at another village, Andy woke up, and realized they had passed by Tawatana. He was in a panic, lest we arrive in Tawatana before him and find him missing. We had no way to contact each other at this point, other than face-to-face, so if I showed up at Tawatana and he wasn't there, he knew I would not be okay. I didn't know anybody, could barely speak reasonable *Solomons Pijin*, and couldn't contact my husband. If he wasn't there, I would imagine the worst, and he knew it. Hurriedly, he got off the ship in the dark of the night, somewhere on the island of Makira, and hired a motorboat to bring him back to Tawatana, fortunately arriving just hours before the kids and I did. The cargo remained on the ship, continued around the island for a while, and eventually was delivered on the return trip.

While, unbeknownst to us, Andy was taking his extended tour of the island by ship and motorboat, the kids and I boarded the *Ocean Express*. The *Express* was originally a riverboat in Malaysia, built for speed. It took 14-24 hours for a cargo ship to get to the village, but the *Express* could do it in a mere 6. The *Express*, while fabulous in the speed category, was a little scant on safety features. We'd heard that the Peace Corps wouldn't let their teams travel on it. Apparently, though, it was okay for missionaries.

The *Express* looked a lot like a torpedo—long, lean, and completely enclosed. All the passengers sat inside, behind sealed windows, in rows of three molded fiberglass seats on each side of a narrow aisle. I think it was the part about being sealed in, that the Peace Corps didn't like. Truthfully, I could understand the Peace Corps' point. It was disconcerting, to say the least.

Friends of ours, who came to visit a few months later, traveled on the *Express* and were given a receipt for freight, misspelled "fright." They agreed that this was indeed an accurate description of the experience. In rough seas, the *Express* rolled so much that alternately, you looked at the sky, then rolled down to look at the sea. You just kept hoping that the boat would roll back up the right way, and not flip completely over.

That first day, though, the seas were fine, and it was kind of fun. We roared away from the wharf and ploughed along the coast of Guadalcanal, air conditioning blasting and Kung Fu movies blaring. Someone came by, selling hard-boiled eggs, and the kids each wanted one. We pulled in at a village wharf, the last stop on Guadalcanal, where everyone bought drinking coconuts and oranges. Lots of people gave food to the little white kids and were just tickled when they ate it. Then we headed for the open water between Guadalcanal and Makira.

About half an hour later, I made my first ship-travel resolution. *Never, ever let anyone eat boiled eggs on a ship.* I've heard that there are two stages of seasickness. First, you are afraid you will die. Then you are afraid you won't. When you are on the receiving end of egg vomit from two small children, both stages pretty much hit simultaneously. The lapful of regurgitated eggs was nastier than words can say. It was, sadly, a harbinger of horrible things to come in my relationship with ocean-going craft of all kinds. Me and ships: we got off to a very bad start, and never managed to reconcile our differences.

After two hours of agony in the open channel between islands, toiling over the big ocean rollers, we reached the coast of Makira, where the bulk of the island created a barrier to the worst of the waves. In protected waters again, with seasickness at bay, I could look out the window and appreciate the vibrant beauty of the jungle, tumbling down cliff edges to meet tiny slivers of sand and enormous outcroppings of black reef-rock at the water's edge. At intervals along the coast, there were towering mushroom-shaped rocks, sliced off from the island and undercut by the relentless tide. The abundant emerald rain forest sprang up on the edge of the sea and ran up the hills and cliff-sides, into the mountainous interior of the island. Spectacularly wild, gorgeously untamed, magnificently pristine, this was a true South Pacific paradise.

We made two stops—Marau Bay, a wide stretch of black sand, and Ubuna, a flat shelf of reef with waves flying into the air. Finally we arrived at Tawatana, where a little creek emptied into the ocean, providing a break in the reef and a sandy beach. The village we called Tawatana was actually a string of little hamlets along the shore, each with their own place-name. Tawatana was the place-name of the beach area where we came ashore. Up the coast, 10 or 15 minutes' walk in either direction from the beach at Tawatana, were numerous clusters of houses, where extended families lived in close proximity to each other. Farther inland were the gardens that each family tended together. We knew that about 500 people lived in the Tawatana area. From the ship, however, we could see only a sliver of beach and a lot of jungle, with very little sign of human habitation. It was like no place we had ever been before, but it was supposed to become home to us.

I zipped the kids into their little life jackets and prepared for the moment I had dreaded so much--handing them over the side of the rolling ship, into the bobbing dinghy. I didn't know it that day, but some of the Melanesian men who stood with hands outstretched to receive Libby and Matt from me would become like family to us, loving and caring for our children as if they were their own. They were also, to a man, far more competent than I would ever hope to be around ships, dinghies, canoes, and salt water vessels in general. I didn't know enough to trust them in that moment, but they were trustworthy anyway.

Tawatana, viewed from the deck of a ship at anchor

We made it into the dinghy safe and sound, and then headed for shore, where a crowd of hundreds had gathered to see the white family arrive. The dinghy rode a wave onto the beach, and the men jumped out to hold it steady. Andy came down to lift the kids out, while I heaved myself overboard and slogged ashore through knee-deep water. As soon as we were on dry ground, everyone crowded around to smile and shake hands. Even the tiniest babies had their little hands offered to us for a miniscule shake. Shaking hands with everyone present was the normal way to greet people in the Solomons, and we had done it on other occasions. This day, however, the more hands I shook, the more deeply I felt the ceremonial significance of joining hands with people I expected to live with for many years to come.

Settling in

Tawatana, October 1993

"Is there a spirituality for the rest of us who are not secluded in a monastery, who don't have it all together and probably never will?" —*Michael Yaconelli*

"I walked far down the beach, soothed by the rhythm of the waves, the sun on my bare back and legs, the wind and mist from the spray on my hair." —*Anne Morrow Lindbergh*

Directly ahead of us when we came ashore the church stood, thatched and sturdy, walls open to the sea breezes. When we had shaken all the hands that we could, we crossed a shallow creek to the east of the church and passed through a small cluster of houses made of sago-palm leaves and split bamboo. The bare, sandy ground around each house was carefully swept clean, a daily chore for the young girls of the family. Outdoor cook houses—simple thatched roofs, supported by posts—sheltered stone ovens where sweet potato, taro, or cassava would be baked later in the day. Bright-leaved plants marked the edge of the path we walked along, and huge, shady trees sheltered us from the tropical sun.

We left the beach, climbed up a steep, rocky path to another small gathering of houses, and finally came to Mr. Ben's house, where we would stay for our first year in the village. The house was high up on concrete pillars, so I could hang laundry underneath, safe from the rain. It was far more comfortable than anything I had expected, boasting an indoor flush toilet, sinks, louvered glass windows, and hardwood floors. It was nicer than the house we would build for ourselves a year later.

The house wasn't quite finished, however, and none of the plumbing was hooked up yet. As a result, we bathed in the creek, carried drinking water to the house in buckets, and rinsed diapers in the sea. We could use the toilet in the house, but then we had to flush with buckets of water, carried up the hill to the house from the sea, and poured into the tank by hand. Consequently, we flushed sparingly, but I was very grateful for any flushing at all.

Mr. Ben's house was a palace, in comparison to our village residence during orientation, and it was a palace in a pristine rain forest setting. The yard was planted in clover, lush and soft and green, surrounded by thick jungle on three sides. The fourth side was a cliff, also heavily forested, dropping down to the sea.

The voice of the sea lay, like the roll of tympani, under the symphony of sounds that composed every day village life. There was always the sound of the sea, sometimes a whisper, sometimes a pounding roar. Above the sea, other sounds came and went. Parrots screeched early in the morning. Roosters crowed. Cicadas sizzled louder and louder as the day warmed up. When it rained—and since we lived in a tropical rain forest, it often rained—the drumming on the tin roof would shut out the rest of the world, and we'd be safely cocooned in our house until the rain passed. In the evening, I prepared dinner to the rhythm of coconuts being scraped next door for sweet potato soup. Late at night, voices told stories around the fire. Pan-pipe bands played, off in the distance, with the sound floating in and out on the breeze as we drifted off to sleep.

After about a week, Andy had installed the solar panels on the roof, hooked up the batteries, and connected our two-way radio. Our only immediate way to contact the world outside Tawatana was the two-way radio. We had no phone, no internet, no email, and no television. We could write letters, but there was no post office. Only ships passing by, every few weeks, would pick up a box of mail for us and carry it to town. Therefore, connecting the radio to the batteries became the very first thing we did when arriving in the village each time, and disconnecting the radio was the last thing we did before we left.

Each day, we'd use the radio to check in with our director back in Honiara, at a scheduled time known as *The Sked*. All the families in our group around the Solomons would turn on their radios at noon each day. There'd be roll-call, and we'd say whether we had any business for the office or not. There would be general business from the office in town, announcements that everyone needed to hear, and news about ships traveling out to various villages. We could ask to talk to other teams, if there was time at the end of *The Sked*. We learned to say "Over" when we were done talking, and "Roger" to acknowledge that we'd heard a message.

The Sked was literally a lifeline, our way to call for help if anything went wrong. It was also an emotional lifeline, a brief connection each day to the off-island world. In later years, I would spend hours each Sunday afternoon chatting with my missionary friends on other islands. It was like the old party line my grandmother had back in Kentucky, though. Anybody anywhere in the country could listen in, and every once in a while, some unknown person would chime in with comments or questions.

Wife, Mother, Neighbor

Once he got Mr. Ben's house fixed up, and our tenuous connection with the outside world established, Andy started language-learning sessions with another man called Ben, who turned out to be a patient teacher and faithful family friend. He spent most of the day out and about with Ben, listening and learning the language.

While Andy was learning language, I was trying to make the household run. My days usually began down at the creek, doing laundry. Scrub. Rinse. Wring. Scrub. Rinse. Wring. As I did this, 4-year-old Libby wandered along the creek with the village kids while 2-year-old Matthew clung desperately to my arm or leg as hard as he could. After an hour or so of washing, it was time for the steep climb up to the house. I carried two buckets of wet clothes and Matthew, while dragging Libby up over the rocks and home again. Then I'd hang the laundry, change into dry clothes, get the kids a snack, and begin working on lunch. If I made bread, it was a three-hour process, with time while the bread rose, to go out and visit the women who lived nearby.

While everyone was friendly, the women were very shy of me. With one or two exceptions, none of the women in the village had ever been to Honiara. They'd never seen a white woman or a white child, much less talked to one. To add to the awkwardness, my name is Kay. Just before we arrived in the village, an old woman named Kei died. That a white woman with practically the same name had shown up, so soon after Kei's death, was pretty spooky business to some people.

Persistently, however, I would go out, carrying my little notebook in which to write new words. Libby would run ahead, looking for new friends, while Matt was on my hip, with his face buried in my neck. I'd approach a cooking house, say hello, and dead silence would fall. I couldn't say anything; they couldn't say anything. Matt would hang onto me and start fussing that he wanted to go home. Then pretty soon it was time to go put the bread in the oven anyway.

All through our training, I had heard how important it was for the wife to "be involved in the project." People said that if the wife wasn't involved in the project, the whole thing would go down in flames. I didn't want to be the reason our project failed, so I had tried hard to prepare myself to be involved with the project.

Early in our training with our organization back in the States, I did some of the linguistics classes we were supposed to do, but truthfully, I hated linguistics. Some fool person had figured out that you can do math with words. A bunch of other people jumped on the bandwagon, and that's how the whole world of linguistics came to be. It was a dark and barren place for me. I loved words, but I did not want to do math with them.

The first semester of classes didn't absolutely kill me, and my grades were pretty good, but then I had a baby. And after being in linguistics class all day, while my baby was in day care, I could not do the six hours of homework that my professors thought was perfectly reasonable.

I hated linguistics. I really, really hated linguistics. And naturally, I wanted to be with my baby.

Andy was very good at linguistics, as he is with all things math-related. From the outset, it was clear that, if we were in linguistic trouble, I would be no help at all. Plus, I wanted to be with my baby. One night I had struggled over a homework problem for several hours. When I went and sat in line for help from the professor's assistant, I was told merely, "You need to look at the data again." The next day, I quit the classes and hung out with my baby and we were all much happier. We realized that we would probably have a fairly traditional home vs. career household when we moved overseas. I'd take care of the home and the kids, and Andy would handle the language project. We felt like that would be fine for us.

Unfortunately, when I told this story to an older lady in the organization, she said to me dispassionately, "Well. You won't be very involved in the project, will you?"

I took that as a statement of disaster, judgment and doom. If I couldn't be involved in the project, there was just no way I could ever measure up!

So four years later, there I was in the village, supposed to be involved in the project. Fortunately, in the Solomon Islands, we had found a country where our local mission group recognized that most of the moms had their hands full, just being moms and trying to keep their families from starving. Nonetheless, some effort was still expected of me toward language-learning, and even I could acknowledge that it was not great to be in this *Arosi*-speaking village, with me cluelessly silenced.

In a kind and just world, all of the effort I'd already put in to learning Papua New Guinea *Tok Pisin*, and *Solomons Pijin*, would have given me some kind of boost when it came to learning *Arosi*. In the real world, though, *Arosi* was an entirely new language. It wasn't terribly difficult grammatically, but it did have tens of thousands of new words, none of which I knew. My math skills were poor, but even I could tell that learning 10 new words a day, a monumental task for me, was a drop in the bucket. At that rate, it would take a couple of years before I could conceivably speak like a toddler. Still, I had to try.

I quickly picked up a few words, like *wai* which means "water." Since we were surrounded by it, *wai* was a word we heard a lot. But then it seemed like I was hearing *wai* even more than I expected. I asked Andy about it. "Why are people ALWAYS saying *wai*? Can they really be talking about water all THAT much?" That's when he told me that *wai* can also be the first person singular word, "I". *Wai* is also a future-tense verb for "to carry" and also means "river" as well as "water."

Grammatically, you could have this sentence: "wai waiwai wai na'i wai." Which means, "I will carry water to the river." Thankfully, no one ever carries water to the river, but they could say it in just this mind boggling way. It was this kind of linguistic math-language mumbo jumbo that made me crazy, when all I wanted to do was get to know my neighbors.

After a few weeks of juggling domestic duties and language study, I hired a girl to do our laundry, and another girl to take care of the kids for an hour each morning, so I could try more formal language lessons.

I started meeting with Ida, who had an Australian sister-in-law, and wasn't intimidated by me at all. Ida was a wonderful language teacher. When I asked her how to say something like, "I am from America," she would tell me how to say it, word for word. Then she would say, "But we never say it that way. We say, I am a woman belonging to America." Then she would teach me how to say that instead. This was exactly the kind of instructor I needed, and I was thrilled to have found her. About three weeks into our lessons, though, she had to quit teaching me so that she could practice every day for the ladies' netball tournament, coming up at Christmas time.

After Ida, Margaret helped me for about three weeks. She was also a good teacher and friend. Soon, though, she had to quit because her mother-in-law wanted her to pick mollusks off the reef, or go to the garden, or do the cooking. In the Solomons, a wife literally belongs to her husband's family, because they have paid a bride-price for her. She is theirs, and she must do what they say.

Then it was Christmas time, when no one works for two or three months anyway. Meanwhile, Andy was having consistent daily lessons with Ben, who had the perfect freedom of a Melanesian man to do exactly as he pleased each day, and it pleased him to teach Andy.

In the end, I never really got language-learning organized. After a number of false starts and failed attempts, I just stuck with what I could reasonably do: I could cook and I could keep the house clean and I could pay attention to my kids. Sometimes we could take a walk and say hi to a few people. After that, the day was over. I felt bad when I had to tell someone that I didn't know much language, but I also felt better on a daily basis, just doing what I could do.

The kids and I learned to walk on the reef at low tide, crouching in shallow water to look at sea urchins and sea stars and tiny electric-blue fish. We found the beaches that were good for shelling, and we learned that if we waited until late afternoon, the sun would sink behind the western mountains so we could walk on the beach in the shade, and a breeze would come up, cooling our skin after the heat of the day. With the sound of the sea crashing all around us, we would find cowries large and small, fragile white sea urchins, empty orange crab shells, bits of driftwood carved into interesting shapes, and pieces of pumice floated in on the tide, from a far away volcano. The beach and everything on it was amazingly, spectacularly beautiful. No billionaire on earth lived in a lovelier place than we did.

Often, our neighbors gave us papayas and bananas and pineapples and sweet potatoes. We made gifts of banana bread, banana fritters, and banana pancakes in return. At moments like that, I had whispers of the sweet, quiet, settled life I was hoping to find after so much upheaval.

Gifts from Off-Island

Every couple of weeks, our group director, Freddy, would box up our snail mail for us. He'd hear of a ship going to Makira, and he'd write "Andy Bruner, Tawatana, Makira" on the box of mail and take it to the ship. Usually he'd find someone coming to Tawatana or maybe to Ubuna, and that person would deliver the mail to our doorstep. Sometimes our director's wife, Bekah, would put a loaf of bread in the box or a bundle of green beans from the market in Honiara.

Mail days were the happiest days, the one time we'd hear from family at home in America. The news was always a month to six weeks out of date, but it was the only news we had. If we knew a box of mail was coming, we'd be listening for the ship's engines all day. On a few sad and terrible days, the ship forgot to stop with our mail. Our precious box would end up someplace further down the island, and then some nice person would bring it up to us. It always got to us eventually, but after waiting two weeks between mail days, the sight of the ship going past with my mail would cast me into despair.

It was on one of those non-stopping-days that Andy first learned to make donuts to compensate for the missing mail. The donuts turned out so well that we kept making them, even when the mail did arrive as scheduled. We found that dessert in general was a good antidote to whatever had happened each day.

At Christmas that year, we got probably the best thing ever delivered to our village by ship: friends. Our friends Pat and Beth, and their girls Claire and Corrie, were brand new to the Solomons, like us. They came out to see what village life was about, and that was that: true love forever. Their girls were close in age to Libby and Matt, and the four of them quickly became the closest thing you can have to cousins, without being actual blood relatives.

Pat and Beth brought with them a huge treat: a Christmas ham from Freddy and Bekah. Bekah had picked it up fresh from the butcher, still warm from the hamming process. So on

Christmas day, I warmed the ham in our little bitty oven, while Beth and I fixed the rest of the meal. We all sat down to eat.

After a few bites, Andy said hesitantly, "I think this ham is raw."

"It can't be raw," I said. "Ham is cooked. It always says on the package, fully cooked ham."

"But it's tough," he said. "Isn't ham supposed to be tender and flaky? I think it's raw."

Confidently, I pulled out *The Joy of Cooking*, to prove that ham is always, by definition, fully cooked. By that time, though, everybody had concluded, regardless of what information *The Joy of Cooking* might offer, that the ham was raw, and they were putting it back in the pan.

Careful perusal of *The Joy of Cooking* revealed that ham could indeed be merely smoked, leaving it partially unfinished. I had to concede that I was mistaken about the fully cooked nature of all ham. Back the ham went into the oven, until it had that nice hammy flakiness that had been so sadly lacking before, and we ended up with ham biscuits for breakfast the next day.

After Christmas, we needed to return to Honiara to buy supplies for our next 3-month village stay. Pat and Beth and their girls couldn't stay with us forever, either, much to our dismay. They would move to another island and start their own language project.

To get back to town, we had planned to go on the *Ocean Express*. However, a tropical depression made the seas too dangerous for the *Ocean Express*, and we ended up instead with tickets on Solomon Airlines, which flew small planes in and out of the provincial capital of Makira, Kira Kira. It was a three-hour motor boat ride down the coast to Kira Kira, and then a 45 minute plane ride back to Honiara.

Looking back, I'm not exactly sure why we thought that an open motor boat would be a better option than a ship in bad weather, even a sketchy vessel like the *Ocean Express*. God saves the foolish, is all I can say about this episode.

Motor boats in our area were 12 to 14 feet long, made of molded fiberglass. For some reason, they were almost always painted orange and turquoise. In the very front was a low, covered area for cargo. The rest of the space was open for passengers, sitting two or three across. The boat driver would sit or stand at the back, manning the outboard motor.

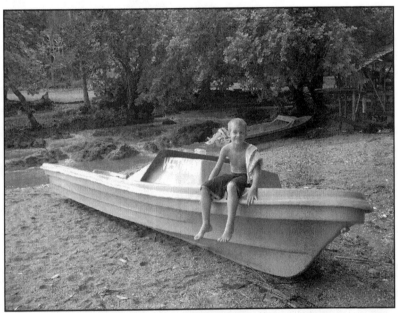

Had the weather been clear, I think it could have been a nice trip. It started drizzling, though, and the wind kicked up. When we got wet, we got cold. We found a tarp and tried holding that over us to keep the rain off. That worked pretty well until a corner came loose and started beating around in the wind, like a flock of Alfred Hitchcock's killer birds. Water started getting into the outboard motor, so instead of skimming over the tops of the waves, we were laboring up one side and falling down the other. At times, the engine would stop all together. The driver would open the engine cover and tinker, while Andy and Pat used the paddles to keep the boat oriented properly to the waves, so we didn't capsize.

Two-year-old Corrie verbalized the misery for us at intervals. She would pull out her pacifier and say, "Cold. Yucky." Then she would barf, moan, and settle back down to wait for the end. By some miracle, we made it alive into Kira Kira in time for the plane, soaked to the skin. One of our fellow passengers confessed that she had needed the ladies' room (conspicuously missing from our little vessel) and in desperation had wet herself. None of us knew. We all looked the same.

Giving birth

Honiara, January to October 1994

"Purposeful giving is not as apt to deplete one's resources; it belongs to that natural order of giving that seems to renew itself even in the act of depletion. The more one gives, the more one has to give—like milk in the breast."—Anne Morrow Lindbergh

"Girlfriend, you're dreaming."—Kay Bruner

While we were in Honiara that January, I got pregnant and I was sick as I never knew it was possible to be sick. The smell of powdered milk made me throw up. The smell of bread made me throw up. The smell of the inside of the kitchen cabinets made me throw up. For the next four months, I threw up. Throwing up was my life. We did not go back to the village as planned, because I was throwing up, though even ships could hardly have made me throw up more.

For my prenatal care, I went to the local clinic with all the other pregnant ladies. On weigh-in days, I took my blue health care booklet and walked down the hill to the clinic building. At least 50 other ladies would be there too. I'd squeeze in through the door and toss my booklet down on the pile. Then I'd wait for my name to be called. When it was time, I'd step up to the table, get weighed and have my blood pressure taken right there in front of everyone. Then it was time for the urine test. Back in America, I'd get a cup in which to present my specimen. Here, I just got that little strip of paper that normally, in America, would have been dipped into the specimen cup. In the Solomon Islands, it was my job to aim well, or wave the paper proficiently, whichever method I preferred, just so the paper got wet like it was supposed to. As the months progressed, and visibility below my waistline diminished, this became an increasingly difficult task.

There were two or three doctors who did prenatal exams, so after the paper and water exercise, I was admitted to the exam room where I'd lie down on one of four tables, all next to each other, with other patients in the process of examination, with my feet facing toward the uncurtained windows with a crowd milling around the shops outside. Fortunately under the circumstances, the doctors never did an internal exam or so much as raised my shirt. They just measured my stomach, told me how far along I was, and sent me home.

When delivery day came, and my contractions were about 3 minutes apart, Andy drove me to the hospital. Doctors don't usually attend births at the Honiara hospital. Nurse-midwives take care of deliveries. One such nurse took my blood pressure and stuck my finger for a malaria slide and took my temperature with a thermometer that smelled like an armpit (not mine). Finally, she showed us to a big room full of beds, and left us there to await developments.

Fortunately, there wasn't anyone else in the labor ward, because Andy's presence was not normal and might have unnerved them. In the Solomons, labor and delivery are traditionally women's work. In fact, not too many years ago, a woman would go into the jungle alone and build a house for herself toward the end of her pregnancy. The women of her family would bring food to her, but she would deliver the baby on her own and stay alone until she stopped bleeding. Birth is believed to be a dangerous time, when the spirits can come and go with ease. It was thought best for a woman to face this alone, rather than endangering others as well as herself and her baby. Even though people went to Christian churches, and these beliefs were no longer overtly taught, it still wasn't normal for a man to be involved in labor and delivery, as Andy was. We were really grateful nobody else was in labor at the time. That seems like a strange circumstance, looking back. The privacy was a little gift of grace in my time of need.

A couple of hours later, I was feeling ready to push, so Andy went out looking for a nurse. At midnight the shift had changed, and he couldn't find anyone inside. Finally he went out in the courtyard where a couple of women were sitting in wheelchairs. "My wife is having a baby in there. Do you know who works here?" "We work here," they said calmly.

They came in, broke my water, and then told me that I couldn't have the baby there in the labor ward. "Don't push! Don't push! We have to walk to the delivery room," they commanded me. Obediently, Andy held me under one armpit, while a nurse held me under the other, and they dragged me, shrieking, down the hall to the delivery room. The wheelchairs, apparently, were not considered necessary for the patient at this point, occupied as they probably were by other employees on break in the courtyard.

Once in the delivery room, I had to climb up into the delivery chair, which was approximately the height of Mount Everest. All the while, I was worried about my dress getting messy, as it was borrowed from a friend. There were no hospital gowns to be had; I never saw a single one while I was there. Not long after my ascent into the chair, Michael was born and immediately placed in a baby warmer under a light. For me, there was a lengthy interval of stitching without anesthetic, during which Andy went and fainted in the corner. Then I had to get down from the chair and walk to the recovery room.

Giving birth

After a short stay in the recovery room, I had to move to the maternity ward, at the far end of the hospital from the delivery ward. It was literally half a city block away, outside and down a covered walkway. After my previous experiences with walking that night, I was grateful to have a wheelchair for that expedition. I remember being shell-shocked and shaky, holding Michael in my arms, as the nurse pushed the wheelchair out into the tropical night and down the walkway, with the sea murmuring away beside us. I was given a semi-private room, which meant two beds instead of twenty. My roommate was a Polynesian woman who had given birth just a few hours before me. Her stomach was already totally flat, and the next morning she was sitting out on the concrete steps chatting with her sisters.

She was my guide to hospital procedure over the next couple of days. I learned that the plate of cold canned spaghetti, accompanied by a hard-boiled egg, was our breakfast. The bucket of warm water outside the door was for the baby's bath. I just needed to haul it inside and pour it into the plastic tub provided for the purpose. The crowd gathered outside meant that it was time for the baby's shots, so we needed to go stand in line. The guy in the soccer shorts who stuck his head in and said, "How are you?" was the doctor, and that my answer of "Fine" meant that I was, in fact, checked out of the hospital and ready to go home.

Settling in ... again

"Cross Jesus one too many times, fail too often, sin too much, and God will decide to take his love back. It is so bizarre, because I know Christ loves me, but I'm not sure he likes me, and I continually worry that God's love will simply wear out." —*Michael Yaconelli*

When Michael was four weeks old, we were on a ship again, headed back to the village. I was still bleeding a little. It was a Monday night, and on the previous Friday I'd had strep throat and a fever of 104. Somehow I had still managed to get everything cleaned, packed, organized and ready to go. I boarded the ship fighting back tears, terrified of getting off the ship on the other end with a baby so tiny.

When I think about all the crazy things we did over the years, taking a four week old baby to the village tops the list. At the time, however, we had not considered that there might be a line between a reasonable level of sacrifice for a good cause, and throwing ourselves under the bus. We heard things like, "The center of God's will is the safest place to be," so we just kept doing the next thing, no matter what. We figured that doing this translation project was in the center of God's will. We both thought that, as long as we stayed strong and kept going, everything would be fine. We didn't think of ourselves as human beings with needs that required self-care. In fact, we had never heard the words "self-care." We thought God would magically take care of us. Or, if He didn't, then we would be like those missionaries in the river in Ecuador, gloriously martyred. In light of that, it was natural to think that it would be selfish to waste time and money on ourselves, waiting in Honiara for me to feel better when I was relatively ambulatory and not barfing any more.

Furthermore, underneath those quasi-religious beliefs, my deep feelings of inadequacy, which required me to perform at any cost, were a beast that never stopped feeding. I constantly had to prove that the project would not fail because of me, and I always felt like I wasn't doing well enough. We had lost almost a year of the project because I couldn't stop throwing up, so we got on the first ship that we could. My anxiety that night was almost overwhelming, yet I kept going.

We were traveling on a cargo ship this time, sleeping all night on the cover of the cargo hold, a platform about 15 feet long and 20 feet wide that we shared with 30 or 40 other passengers. We had two single-size inflatable camping mattresses, which all five of us shared. Other people were asleep on simple woven mats, or on the bare boards. One young man was even asleep on a pile of corrugated roofing iron. By contrast, our thin mattresses were luxurious. A lady in a pink shirt spent most of the night trying to edge her way onto my mattress. Likewise, I spent most of the night with my knees planted in her back, trying to edge her back off my mattress. I didn't want her rolling over onto baby Michael.

Wife, Mother, Neighbor, Teacher

Somehow we made it through the night, arriving once again in Tawatana. Our new house, much simpler and smaller than Mr. Ben's house, was almost ready for occupancy. During the very first weeks of my pregnancy with Michael, two of my brothers and a family friend had come out to the Solomons and spent a week in Tawatana, helping Andy get the house framed and roofed. Later, Andy had taken a brief trip out to Tawatana to put the exterior walls in place, while I stayed behind in Honiara and threw up. When we arrived back in Tawatana as a family, we spent a few weeks at Mr. Ben's house while Andy put final touches on the interior.

The exterior walls of our new house were made of locally-sawn timber, while the interior walls were thin wall boards or panels of sewn sago leaf. In an attempt to help the heat rise and dissipate, there was no ceiling, just open space under the tin roof, where the attic would traditionally be. Consequently, there was very little privacy. As the kids got older, Andy and I would be talking about something in our bedroom, only to have a little head pop over the wall as someone stood up on the top bunk next door to offer insight into the conversation. We found that if we wanted to talk about something privately, we had to take a walk outside to do it.

A water tank, mounted on a tall stand outside the kitchen window, allowed water to gravity-feed into the house, so we could have an indoor toilet and a kitchen sink. Andy installed a showerhead under the tank so we could shower at home, rather than going down to the creek. This was much more convenient, though I still had to wear a sarong as my own personal shower curtain, and attempt to wash discreetly beneath it. I really hated opening my eyes after shampooing my hair, to find that an audience had formed for my next bizarre ritual: the shaving of my armpits.

Michael was born the day after Libby's fifth birthday, and Libby knew that when you turned five, you started school. So in addition to a newborn and a toddler, I had a very determined kindergartener on my hands. I was given a curriculum to follow, but pretty soon I suspected that it was a bad match for Libby and me. We were supposed to do a "three-pass reading method." I was supposed to read a story aloud, then we would read it together, and then she would read it on her own. According to this method, it didn't really matter if she made mistakes. The key was just to try, and eventually she would figure it out. According to Libby, however, I was not teaching her properly. She knew she didn't know how to read, and she wasn't going to try until I taught her.

Fortunately, somebody recommended a phonetics program called *Sing, Spell, Read, and Write,* which taught letter sounds by pointing at pictures and singing a little song that will be stuck in my brain until my dying day. "A-a-apple, b-b-ball . . ." This turned out to be an acceptable instructional method to Libby, and she quickly learned to read.

Libby and Matthew, at ages 5 and 3, were now both old enough by village standards to run with a pack of friends. There were always adults outside keeping an eye on the kids, because in Melanesian households, the only thing done indoors was sleeping at night. Cooking was done outside, chores were all outside, chatting with family and friends was done outside. The kids were never completely unsupervised. However, there was also no one "designated adult watching the children" like I was used to. While I hated not knowing where my kids were at all times, that was the village way, and I just tried to trust it.

Over time, we came to see that our children occupied pretty much the upper stratosphere of society when we were with Pacific Islanders. People would give my children anything—anything—that they asked for.

One day in Honiara, Libby came inside with a big green drinking coconut in her hand. I knew we didn't have any coconuts around right then, so I asked where she'd gotten it.

"From a lady by the school," she said. The local elementary school was across the street from our house. "She had two. She knew I wanted this one. She kept the other one for herself," she explained.

"How did she know you wanted it?" I asked.

"I went over and held out my hand."

In Tawatana, I would look out my window and see that my neighbor was cooking a pot of sweet potato soup in the middle of the morning, which was not her normal soup-cooking time. When I spotted my kids over there, I'd go over and say, "Hey, Ireen! You're cooking at a funny time?"

She would sheepishly say, "Michael's really hungry."

Now, I love my children and I think they are great, but it took me quite a while to understand what prompted everyone else to treat them with so much indulgence.

The biggest factor was the fundamentally different way that Islanders looked at life. We Westerners saw a linear progression of birth into a nuclear family, followed by a childhood of training toward independent adulthood, then independent adulthood, and finally death, which we tried to think about as little as possible.

Islanders, however, had a much more cyclical view of life. They believed that a child's spirit arose from the spirit world to be born into a human community, where every uncle was called "father" and every aunt was called "mother." In addition, children were called by the exact same kinship term as they used to address their elders. For example, a daughter called her mother and aunts *nanai*, and the mother and aunts called the daughter *nanai*. These reciprocal terms of address reflected the reality that this was a culture that valued egalitarian relationship over hierarchy. When they passed through puberty, children were welcomed into a community of adults who worked together for survival and companionship. At the end of life, everyone would pass into the community of ancestral spirits, who had power to make gardens succeed or fail, and to cause health or illness.

In this system, everyone in the community felt connected to, and responsible for, everyone else's child. Furthermore, everyone had a vested interest in each child's future as a community member, and then as an ancestral spirit. This egalitarian style between parents and children included a great deal of freedom for the children. My kids had all that going for them, and then they had white skin, which made their status even higher.

The Solomon Islands didn't have the sad history of wholesale slavery and colonial oppression that other nations had suffered. Churches had been established by white missionaries who had a fair amount of respect for local customs, bringing in schools and medical care. In our area, a beloved Anglican priest had spent so much time in villages with local people that he became known as "Father Homeless." Even World War 2 had resulted in a positive view of white people, as American and Australian soldiers had worked closely with local communities, and left behind an infrastructure still in constant use. We were still driving on the roads and using the hospital that white skinned soldiers had built.

My childhood experience was in Nigeria, a country that had suffered incredible oppression under European domination. Even as a young child, I knew that my white skin was a problem for local people. I remember riding to kindergarten, clinging to the back of my dad's Honda 90, and people would throw up their hands toward us. I had to learn not to wave back, because the hand motion was not a greeting but a curse, and if we waved back, we were cursing them in return. As missionaries in Nigeria, we lived inside our compound walls, because it often was not safe for us to be outside. In the Solomons, though, we were welcome in the community.

I know we were a strange little family to their community. No other adults acted like we did. While everybody else in the village worked their gardens, fished from the reef, and sat around cooking fires late into the night, Andy worked on learning language, and I stayed inside my house, teaching my children and cooking. With the high risk for malaria, we did not sit around outside in the dark. We sat inside at night, under our single 2-foot fluorescent light, and read books aloud to each other. Regardless of these odd behaviors, people were disposed to think well of us, and to treat us kindly. The real stars of the show, though, were our kids, who ran around and did things that kids were supposed to do. They assimilated themselves, despite the differences in culture.

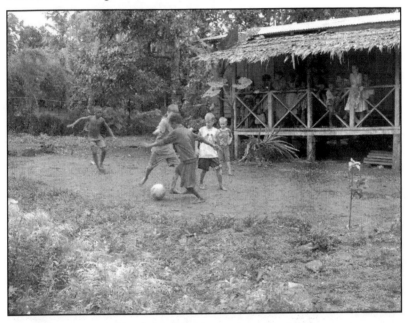

Our house in Tawatana, with the usual suspects at play (2002)

As the village kids got to know us, our porch became Disneyland, Tawatana. We had a bucket of crayons and lots of paper off-cuts from the printing press in town for art projects. We had a small library of childrens' books that lived out on our front porch, which were endlessly fascinating to the neighborhood kids, and even to the adults who dropped by. When we had tempura paint or colored chalk, the kids all loved to create art on the concrete shower-pad under our water tank. As the kids got older, they played endless games of Dutch Blitz with their friends, resulting in ruthless card skills for all.

Our kids learned to play all kinds of village games, too. *Five stone* was kind of like jacks, with stones being tossed and picked up in certain patterns. *In water* was a tag game, played along lines drawn in the dirt. There were also seasonal game-fads, based on whatever plants were currently producing fruit. When the bush apples were tiny and green, the kids would make pop guns with hollow bamboo, using the bush apples as ammunition. When it was time to plant a yam garden, they played the kokoriki juggling game. The noise of the kokoriki nuts clicking together, and the accompanying song, would encourage the yams to grow quickly.

The village kids were responsible for their own snacks during the day, so finding fruit and cracking nuts occupied much of their time. They liked to come over to our house with a handful of nuts or a papaya, and ask our kids to contribute a precious pack of ramen noodles, so they could all build a fire and cook in the yard.

Some of the adults in the village eventually told us, "We'd like to come and see you, but you always have so many kids at your house. It's too noisy over there."

Wife, Mother, Neighbor, Teacher, Invalid

After Michael was born, I started having strep throat about every six weeks, and I just couldn't seem to stay well. If I didn't have strep throat, I'd have something else. One time I developed a fine rash all over my body, and my eyes hurt so badly that I couldn't open them. While describing the symptoms to a friend over the radio, she said it sounded like dengue fever, a mosquito-borne tropical disease. I was flat out in bed for several weeks and, for the only time in my life, couldn't summon the energy to hold a book open.

Even worse, the kids got sick. Malaria. Conjunctivitis. Tropical ulcers. Never mind the weird things I couldn't figure out. One time, the night before we were supposed to get on the ship to go back to Honiara, Libby started breathing strangely. By the time we got back to town, she was sleeping all the time and wheezing horribly. We drove directly from the wharf to the doctor, who diagnosed pneumonia and sent her straight to the hospital where she spent the night on oxygen and antibiotics.

Whenever we were in the village, I continually feared that somebody was going to die and that there would be nothing I could do about it, and it would be my fault. I started waking up a lot at night, fear-stricken, with racing thoughts, not being able to get back to sleep. I had nightmares about sharks, crocodiles, and falling coconuts. Every time one of the kids had a fever, I just knew they would be dead by morning.

As time went on, and I kept getting sick, I could barely keep up with the house and teaching the kids, and I fell woefully behind on language learning. Ironically, though, I knew enough to understand people saying, "Andy speaks the language really well, but Kay can't say anything."

While my physical health failed, my personality seemed to turn against me as well. As an extrovert, living in the village for months at a time, with the kids and my anxieties for company, I would grow fairly desperate for the need to verbally process all that was on my mind. When I got out to speak with other women in the village, my vocabulary was so limited that I couldn't say anything meaningful. I wanted to talk about what was on my heart, and all I could say were things like, "I am going to the beach," and "That is a very big pig."

Andy, on the other hand, spent all day out in the village, talking. As an introvert, by the end of the day, he was ready to close up shop, read a book, and say nothing until tomorrow. I would try to strike up conversations, but he was so tired of conversation that he couldn't summon the capacity to talk with me. We had always had always enjoyed talking together. It was one of the reasons we'd fallen in love, and now it was slipping away.

I remember crying and saying, "Can't we just talk for ten minutes every day?"

Andy would respond, "About what?"

I felt so uninvited—that horrible old feeling from childhood, not being good enough, not being interesting enough, not being wanted. I stopped trying to talk. I just kept it inside.

The separation that grew between us looked normal in the village. Married couples did not do things together. They didn't sit with each other in church, they didn't talk to each other socially, they never held hands or indicated any kind of intimacy in public. We moved to Tawatana in 1993. Ten years later, in 2003, I still did not know who was married to whom, except for the families who lived right around our house. There were simply no obvious signs of marital affection or relationship.

The whole time we lived in the Solomons, we could not touch each other in public. I wasn't allowed to reach out and hold my husband's hand. In private, the constant heat and humidity was not conducive to much physical contact, either. We had sex sometimes, with a fan pointed straight at us. But sitting on the couch with our arms around each other was sticky and gross. There was no snuggling, no hand-holding, no casual touching. It was one more thing that made life lonelier for me.

I had expected my childhood background of life overseas to protect me somehow from the worst of the cultural adjustments, and perhaps it helped somewhat. I had not, however, anticipated how the tropical illnesses and the heat and the loneliness and the pressure of providing the safest, happiest life possible for my family would impact me emotionally and physically. I constantly felt alone, and inadequate for the challenges.

I eagerly anticipated our visits to Honiara, mainly because of the company of the other missionaries. We tried to coordinate Honiara visits so that we overlapped with our friends as much as possible. I remember getting off the boat and making a beeline for Beth's kitchen, where I would stay, talking and talking, for several days straight, until I could decompress a little from all the isolation of the past three or four months in Tawatana.

There was no outside entertainment in Honiara, so we missionaries made our own fun together. We had people over for dinner. We played games. We went to the beach together. Arrivals and farewells were a routine part of life, as people came and went from their village allocations and from their passport countries. We celebrated every transition with a gathering of whoever happened to be in town at the time. As time went on, the farewells mounted and became more painful, as each departure added to the load of losses I carried.

Once or twice a month, on a Sunday night, we would have "Sing and Share" services, where we'd gather to sing worship songs and pray. Usually there were enough ladies around so that we'd be able to meet one morning each week for Bible study. Every time we were in town, I felt like a squirrel storing away nuts for the winter. We'd go to the village and I'd be okay for a while, living on the excess of companionship I'd had in town.

Wife, Mother, Neighbor, Teacher, Invalid, Exhausted

After another year of village life and ship travel, homeschooling and cooking, 1995 rolled around unceremoniously. Andy had conquered the language enough to begin translation work. A couple of local men produced first drafts, while Andy checked their work and mentored them through the translation process. I was just beginning to emerge from the baby-and-home school fog enough to start thinking about language-learning again. I made some simple books with photos cut from Solomon Airlines magazines, and asked the neighborhood kids for sentences to describe the photos. I wrote down what they said, and the kids "read" it back to me. They began to think about reading in their own language, and I picked up some of that language at the same time.

While there was a school in the village, which all the children attended, the kids were taught to read in English, a language they didn't even speak. Later on, they would try to use their English decoding skills to read the Arosi prayer book and hymnal, which meant that most people couldn't fluently read the little bit of material that existed in the language they DID speak. We hoped that one day, everybody would learn to read Arosi, their mother-tongue, first and then move on to reading other languages if they wanted.

Sometime in 1995, Andy realized that sitting at a computer, checking first drafts of the translation, was going to be the short road to insanity for him. Unlike his construction job in Tennessee, which kept him busy and happy, a desk job made him stir crazy. He needed a more active, more varied set of tasks each day. He needed more challenges. He told me how he felt about it, and asked me what I thought of him becoming the deputy director of our group, where there would be plenty of new things happening, all the time. We could finish up our first three-year term overseas, Andy said, and when we returned, he could begin the deputy director job. Dutifully I said yes, but inside I was shrieking, "NO! NO! NO!"

Much as I enjoyed being in Honiara with our missionary friends, I did not at all want to be in administrative work. I'd seen good friends become really burned out doing administrative work. I'd seen the kind of demands made of them and their families, and I knew I couldn't do all that, with my three small children. I felt like I was just beginning to find my feet in the village, and I hated the thought of changing the barely-found order of my life yet again.

Worst of all, I knew that taking up the deputy job would not change my life for the better. I would still have to home school the kids and cook and keep up the house. I would just have to add more group-service work, shopping and making life more bearable for the village teams. I knew those things were important, and I deeply appreciated what other people had done to keep me sane in the village, sending out my mail and green beans. Every one of those tasks, however, was a drain to my energy. I wasn't doing anything I felt gifted to do. I was simply doing what had to be done for the sake of the project, and other people's projects. Just as Andy knew that sitting at a computer was not the right job for him, I knew that my work wasn't ideal for me, either. I didn't see any way out of any of my jobs, though. He could change his life, but I just had to put up with mine.

I didn't know how to say no, so I said yes. When I put my "no" away, however, a big boulder of anger went into the box, where the loneliness and inadequacy already lived.

I had a mental picture of myself, alone in a dugout canoe, far from shore. The canoe was riding low, loaded with all kinds of cargo, so that water was about to rush in over the edges. I was paddling as hard as I could, but the current was against me and I could never get any closer to shore. Every so often, a plane would fly overhead and drop another load into the canoe. Everything in that canoe was vitally important, and it was all up to me to get it ashore. I was terrified of tipping the canoe, terrified of it going down. There was nothing I could do but keep paddling, alone and afraid and far from shore.

In May 1996, we returned to the States for a year, to visit family and to report to our team of churches and financial supporters. I kept on paddling that year, too. I was pregnant with our fourth child and teaching a linguistics class at a local college. Me, teaching linguistics. Oh, the irony!

I taught right up to the very day Jacob was born in November, conveniently at the end of the fall semester. I planned to take the spring semester off after that, to just be at home with Michael and Jacob while Libby and Matt went to the local elementary school. At the last minute, I was asked to teach another class in the spring term, and it never occurred to me to say no.

I had discovered that I liked teaching college-level students. Kindergarten was not my thing, but teaching college? I liked that a lot, particularly because it had been so long since I had done anything I felt good at. I didn't want to say no when presented with the opportunity. Moreover, I thought it was my job to make people happy, and I couldn't stand to disappoint anybody. Plus, if somebody else asked me to do something, it was probably the will of God anyway. And who could say no to that? Not me.

So I just kept paddling.

Settling in . . . again

Honiara, August, 1997

"The point of our crises and calamities is not to frighten us or beat us into submission, but to encourage us to change, to allow us to heal and grow." —Kathleen Norris

We returned to the Solomon Islands in 1997 with four children. Andy's new role as deputy director meant that we moved to the capital town of Honiara, rather than going back and forth between Honiara and Tawatana. Andy had his new job in group administration, in addition to the Arosi translation project, which he would manage from a distance.

We bought a small house for ourselves, and created an above-ground pool for the kids using a chopped-off water tank, about 8 feet across and 3 feet deep. My brother and sister-in-law sent the kids a zipline for Christmas, and we strung it up across the back yard so the kids could whizz along it and drop into the pool.

Libby, Matt, Michael, and Jacob quickly made friends in the neighborhood, and once again our yard became play central. The pool was often so full nobody could move in the water. The children built cook fires under the trees, and made noodle soup for snack. Our house was on short pillars, with fine sandy dust underneath. The boys and their friends buried innumerable toy cars and plastic army men, playing for endless hours in the shade under the house.

Among the missionary families we worked with, all the adults were called "aunt" and "uncle." Our kids all ran tame through each other's houses, and sleepovers were the big deal. The rule was, you had to be potty trained, and then you could sleep over. Hardly a weekend passed without some extra children at our house, and one or more of our kids traded off to another family.

We had access to the produce market in town and the daily wonder of fresh bread from the bakery. We had medical care, of sorts, when we needed it. There were even a couple of thrift stores I could poke around in for "new" clothes. No two ways about it, town life was much easier than village life had been. It was also a whole lot busier.

Andy thoroughly enjoyed his deputy director role, which was one challenge after another. Which ship was going where? When? Why wouldn't the cash box balance? Which house had a plumbing problem? Which group vehicle had a flat tire or a busted fuel pump? Where should we put a new driveway to better access the group storage unit? Would there be space for a basketball court, if the driveway ran just so? He was master of our missionary universe and loving it.

My job, meanwhile, was to home school Libby and Matt, while keeping up with a toddler, Michael, and a baby, Jacob.

If I had only had my family to look after, it might have felt manageable. However, I was also the group hostess, which meant 10 to 12 hours' work each week, sewing curtains and couch covers, shopping for incoming families, listening to radio skeds, and supervising the national ladies who cleaned the group houses. We also had guests in for meals frequently, which meant that I was cooking all the time. Our family record for sharing meals in our home was 8 meals in 6 days. At the end of that particular week was Matt's birthday. He begged to please have a family-only party, and we ate out at a hotel in town.

I hired a local lady to come in and help me each day with the housework. She hung the laundry on the line early each morning. She helped keep Michael and Jacob occupied while I taught Libby and Matt. She kept the house clean, inside and out, for our non-stop flow of dinner guests. Since we had no dishwasher, she did the previous night's dishes after we'd had company over.

I felt way too busy and overwhelmed most of the time, and I had never wanted to do this job to begin with. I felt like everybody got a big piece of Andy except for me. I felt alone and abandoned, less important than other people.

I'd been raised on the Sunday School idea that went like this: "Jesus, then Others, then You: what a wonderful way to spell JOY!" Jesus and Others were getting a lot of attention, but it seemed like I never got what I needed, and the JOY was conspicuously absent. I kept doing the Jesus and Others thing anyway, hoping that someday, somehow the JOY would show up. By this time, however, I had been at this method for years and it wasn't working well. I started to wonder if I should try other solutions.

I got a copy of *Boundaries* by Henry Cloud and John Townsend, and I recognized myself as the angry, put-upon person who says yes when she should be saying no. I was pretty sure that it was too late to go back and undo my "yes" to the deputy job, so I just tried to put little boundaries up wherever I could.

I thought that if I said, "I'd rather not," as an expression of my boundaries, other people would understand and back off, but that didn't happen like I hoped. I said, "I'd rather not" and other people said, "You must," and then I did. Whenever I got close to somebody else's hurt, disappointment, or anger, I would fold. Then, I would be hurt, disappointed, and angry instead.

Of course I didn't say much, but all that emotion would leak out, mostly as frustration with Andy, because I blamed him for getting me into this mess. In addition, although I had been healthy while we were in the States, I now started back into the cycle of strep throat every 6 weeks.

Andy would sometimes travel out to visit other teams in their villages, and one evening before he headed out on a ten-day trip, he and I went for dinner at a nice hotel. While we were eating, I started talking about how hard things had been for me lately, and the feeling I had that I wasn't doing very well. He looked at me across the dinner table and said, "At least you're not being burned at the stake." I had been leaking frustration at him for a while, and he was sick of hearing it, so he shut me down.

I was stunned into silence that night, and happy to see him go off on his trip the next day. It took the full ten days before I was prepared to speak to him again. After he returned, we smoothed things over, each of us saying a simple "I'm sorry," and moving on.

Andy took a scuba certification course, and I was all for it, having a romantic picture in my mind of us having fun at the beach, as a family. Our favorite beach was Bonegi, where a

World War 2 ship had been wrecked on a sand bar. All of the wood from the ship had long since rotted away, leaving the iron shell as a spectacular aquarium in shallow water. At low tide, we could walk out to the ship, float over the side, and snorkel for hours over a rainbow of reef and tropical fish.

I pictured the scuba situation as me and the kids in the shallow water, with Andy exploring the depths where none of the rest of us wanted to go anyway. It would be all of us, together, having fun. I think we did that once, and it wasn't as much fun as I'd thought, since I was trying to make sure four kids didn't drown themselves while Andy was off diving. After that, he went out with other dive buddies.

In theory, it was a good thing for him to have a hobby, something fun to do after a long week at the office. In practice, it was one more thing for me to resent, because I'd had a long week at my office too, only to find myself in the same circumstances again, all weekend, alone. I remember him leaving on a scuba trip one Saturday morning with me pounding on the door of the van, yelling at him about something. Neither of us remembers what the problem was that day. I just remember that he drove away. He just remembers that he was really happy to go.

I started having repetitive dreams, where Andy had disappeared, and the kids and I were living happily in Tennessee. There was no violence. I didn't know how he had disappeared. He was just gone. And I was happy.

The beginning of change

Honiara, May 1998

"For as long as you can remember, you have been a pleaser, depending on others to give you an identity. But now you are being asked to let go of all these self-made props and trust that God is enough for you." — Henri Nouwen

"Define yourself radically as one beloved by God. This is the true self. Every other identity is illusion." — Brennan Manning

One Saturday morning, Andy went to the office and I was home writing personal notes on newsletters to our supporters. We'd rented the group TV and VCR for the weekend, and the kids were watching cartoons. From my spot at the kitchen table, I could hear a strange noise in the living room, but I couldn't see the kids around the corner of the room. "What's that funny noise?" I asked. No one answered. "Hey, you guys, what is that noise?" Still no one said anything. I got up and walked into the living room, and there was 9-year-old Libby, eyes rolled back in her head, foam coming from her mouth, making this bubbling noise. The boys were looking at her, motionless and stunned.

I immediately thought that she was choking on the banana she had just been eating, so I tried the Heimlich maneuver. Nothing. I put her down on the floor and tried to get stuff out of her mouth. Nothing. By that time, I was literally screaming out to God to stop it. I thought she was dying, and I couldn't do anything to help. It was my very worst nightmare, coming true right before my eyes. I carried her into the kitchen while 7-year-old Matt picked up the phone, trying to call Andy at the office.

In that moment, I had one of those out of body experiences that you always hear about. I was down on the floor trying to help Libby, and this other part of me stepped out to the side, stood just by the kitchen table about three feet away, and very calmly said, "Right now you have four children, and in a minute you will only have three."

She was limp then, but still breathing. I picked her up and carried her outside, intending to drive somewhere for help. Andy had taken the car to work that day, so I just stood there screaming in the driveway, hoping someone would come and help me. I'll never know how long that episode actually lasted. It seemed like years. Eventually she started to come around, and Andy arrived home with the car. I ran to the car, still barefooted, still carrying her, and we drove to the hospital. On the way, she murmured a few words to me, and I noticed that she was paralyzed on one side. I thought she had had a stroke, or had been oxygen deprived from choking for so long.

When we arrived at the hospital, I ran inside with her and the nurse on duty came up with a thermometer to take her temperature, assuming she had malaria. "Where's the doctor, where's the doctor?" I was yelling.

"Oh, he's over on the other side," she replied, still shaking the mercury down in the old-fashioned thermometer.

I laid Libby down on a nearby stretcher and ran for the doctor myself. The doctor came right away, and concluded that she had had a seizure. Seizures don't kill people, he told me flatly, and there wasn't anything the hospital could do, except observe her overnight. The paralysis was a temporary side effect of the seizure, and within an hour or so, she was back to normal, although very tired.

Libby and I stayed in the hospital overnight. She slept and I lay awake in the narrow bed with her, keeping watch.

The next day we went home and I still didn't sleep. On Monday, Andy went back to work. Presumably, life was supposed to be back to normal.

She continued to have seizures over the next couple of years. Horribly, a lot of her seizures were partial seizures, so she was actually conscious—and terrified—during them. Her seizures were connected to her sleep patterns, so she often had a seizure about 2 hours after she fell asleep.

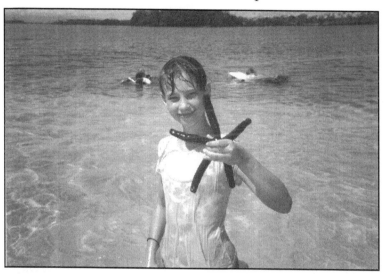

As a result, she was scared to go to sleep, because then she might wake up and have a seizure. However, if she didn't go to sleep, she was more likely to have a seizure as a result of sleep deprivation. The only way she felt safe to sleep was if I sat outside her door every night, listening for the noise she made when she had a seizure. If I heard it, I'd go in and sit with her while she had the seizure and talk her through it. Every time she had one, the muscles in her face changed and distorted and she looked like a different person, like someone dying. It was the most horrible, out-of-control thing I could imagine—even to this day.

Andy appeared completely stoic to me during each of these episodes. One night during a seizure I screamed at him, "What is the MATTER with you? How can you be so calm?"

He replied evenly, "Well, I know it's going to be over in a few minutes, and I know it's not really hurting her, and in fact I think some good will come of it."

I took Andy's composure to be an expression of real faith, in contrast to my lack of composure and total faith failure.

In the midst of this, our group had a conference. The visiting speaker's theme was "God delights in you." I remember sitting there, almost in pieces, listening and thinking, "I should believe that, but I really don't."

I was coming to understand that I had a pretty screwed up belief system. I believed that God could only love good people, and I was falling off the good people wagon in a big way. My faith didn't work, I wasn't happy, I got sick all the time. I wasn't good enough, and because of my inadequacies, I was being punished. My problem was, I couldn't figure out how to be any better.

I was doing the absolute best things I could think of doing. I was being a missionary. I was giving up my husband, not only to a language project but also to administrative work. I was homeschooling my kids. I was helping other missionary families in our group. Yet, what had I gotten in return? I thought of that day in the living room, looking down at Libby seizing. The ONE time I had screamed out to God for something, He had ignored me.

My conclusion in that moment of panic was: God hates me and is punishing me. I have tried, and tried, and tried. I have been the best person I know how to be, but clearly I don't measure up. God must hate me, because look what He is doing. How many stories have I heard of missionaries getting exactly the right miracle at the right time? Why can't I get it to work? God must hate me.

But the Bible says He delights in me.

I could see that something was wrong with my belief system. For one thing, it wasn't working. My "faith" and my performance simply weren't doing what I wanted them to do. Then, too, my feeling that God hated me was in direct conflict with what the Bible said. I started trying to believe that God did indeed love me—maybe even like me—but it was an uphill battle.

I would lay in bed at night and cried helplessly. Andy would offer, "We don't have to stay here. We can leave if you want to."

And I always said, "No, because I will just take this problem with me. If I can't fix it here, I can't fix it anywhere."

The story goes that if you put a frog in a pot of hot water, it will jump right out. But if you put the frog in a pot of cold water, and then gently heat it over a low flame, the frog will sit right there, contentedly boiling to death. I was that proverbial frog, simmering away on the stove. Even when offered the chance to hop out, I wouldn't. I was not going to quit. Failure was not going to be my fault.

At that same time, I went to Bible study every week and regularly confessed that I just couldn't make sense of the Bible, and my prayers didn't seem to be going anywhere. One morning, I was out with a friend from this group and she asked me how it was going with God and me.

I said honestly, "Still not really speaking to each other."

Then she said, very gently, "Have you thought about unforgiveness? I find that when I get into this state, a lot of times it's because I haven't forgiven someone. So do you think you could have unforgiveness in your life?"

"I don't think so," I responded. "But, I'll think about it."

She was a good friend to me and had been praying with me for months, so I felt compelled to honor her courage and to think about it. I started thinking about it right then, at about 10 in the morning. That night I couldn't sleep, and at about 2 o'clock the following morning, I finally admitted how angry I was with Andy about taking on the deputy director work in addition to our translation project. He wanted to change his job, which I agreed to, but consequently, I was incredibly angry with him, because I had felt so trapped in my own jobs.

I woke him up to tell him that I would forgive him for doing something I had agreed that he should do. I apologized for being so angry and mean. During the conversation that followed, Andy told me how, over the span of our marriage, he had grown to hate discussions with me because, when we disagreed, he felt like he couldn't compete verbally. Over time, his solution was to stay out of conversations with me. I told him how tired and lonely I felt, and how much I needed him to engage with me. Afterward we felt more at peace with each other, more connected than we had in several years.

For me personally, that little bit of honesty, of taking responsibility for my own choices, and letting the anger go, started to set my world straight. Just like my friend had said, letting go of unforgiveness enabled me to make sense of my Bible again. I went on a search through scripture that ended in Hebrews 11. I came to those verses at the end of the chapter that talk about those heroes of the faith who were beaten and sawn in two and hidden in caves—those martyrs of the faith— of whom the world was not worthy. These people had such great faith, and yet their lives, if I looked at the outward results, were a disaster. God delighted in them, in their faith, and still He let this horrible stuff happen.

In some weird way, that broke through to me. Just because my life was a mess and I couldn't make it better, didn't mean God hated me. He delighted in those martyrs. He delights in me. I started to think that maybe his love was not about me doing everything just right in order to get what I want. Maybe it was about Him loving me—and Him loving me in His way, not according to my plan, and not as a corollary to my behavior.

A little light began to shine on my internal landscape, and Libby began taking some medication that controlled the seizures. As she slept better, I got more rest. My world began to be a better place.

Once I started to listen honestly to what was in my head, other revelations emerged. One day I was walking down the street when this thought came to me: "Everything I love to do is useless." This stopped me in the middle of the sidewalk. What did I really love to do? Make things pretty, write poetry, have tea with friends. Useless things, I'd always thought. What would be useful? Translating the Bible, saving people, fighting disease and world hunger. Things I was not good at. I started to realize I had denigrated God's gifts to me. I had tried to force myself to be something I was not, at the same time belittling the contributions I could offer. I started to wonder what life would look like if I could do the things I loved.

As I started to be more honest and open with myself, there were days when I still felt out of sorts. Instead of pushing my thoughts and feelings away like I always had before, I would try to understand why I was feeling the way that I felt. One Sunday morning, I wasn't doing well emotionally, and I knew it. Andy took the kids to church while I stayed home to pray and think and journal. My prayer that morning went something like this: "God, something is wrong with me. I don't know what it is. Please show me."

I had one of those experiences where I randomly opened my Bible, and God seemed to speak directly to me. I started reading in Malachi, and came across these verses:

"You have said terrible things about me," says the Lord. "But you say, 'What do you mean? How have we spoken against you?' You have said, 'What's the use of serving God? What have we gained by obeying his commands or by trying to show the Lord Almighty that we are sorry for our sins?'" (Malachi 3: 13,14)

As I read those verses, it struck me how much I expected things to go well for me, in light of all I was doing for God. I could totally relate to the people who said, "What's the use?"

I realized that I had had a certain idea of the sacrifices I would be required to make for the project. I wanted the Abraham-and-Isaac kind of sacrifice. God asked Abraham to sacrifice Isaac, and when Abraham proved he was willing, God stopped him and provided the ram in the thicket instead. I wanted to say, "Yes, Lord," and then to have the sacrifice stop.

It wasn't working out like that, though. I couldn't find that ram in the thicket anywhere. Instead, I was wandering like the Children of Israel, lost in a desert of details, wondering when I would get out of the wilderness and into the land flowing with milk and honey.

"Hello, Pillar of Fire. Let's move it along. This is not going the way that I want. If this is all there is, what's the use?" I could just hear myself saying that. I knew that was in my head.

Then I read these verses:

Then those who feared the Lord spoke with each other, and the Lord listened to what they said. In his presence a scroll of remembrance was written to record the names of those who feared him and loved to think about him. "They will be my people," says the Lord Almighty. "On the day when I act, they will be my own special treasure." (Malachi 3: 16,17)

Here was the invitation that I longed for: to speak, and to be welcomed, to know that God was listening, and was longing to hear all I had to say. God understood that I was trying to work my way through my troubles. I didn't want to give up. I didn't want to be bitter. I wanted to love him. God got it. He knew. What's more, he treasured and delighted in me for speaking about it.

As I had these various experiences of God's love and care, I felt so much better. Lighter. Freer. Happier. It seemed that a change in my thinking was really all that I needed in order to have everything fixed just right, and I was really pleased to arrive at this new place of peace.

Change continues

Honiara, January 1999

"But now — although it may be some time before you are comfortable doing so — it is time for you to let go of it. Your old life is over. No matter how much you would like to continue it or rescue it or fix it, it's time to let go." — William Bridges

Right about the time that Libby got her medication and seizures stopped being such a crisis, we started hearing about a group called the Guadalcanal Revolutionary Army. The name made us laugh, because we just couldn't imagine a revolutionary army in the sleepy little Solomon Islands. It turned out to be no joke. An opposing group was formed — the Malaita Eagle Force — and between them, the GRA and the MEF made quite a mess of what had always been called The Happy Isles.

There were rapes, and killings, and villages burned out on the plains. Our house was on a ridge so we heard automatic weapons firing from all around. Most of the skirmishes took place outside of town, but occasionally there were roadblocks in the area, which were easily achieved by chopping a coconut tree down to fall across the road. When that happened, we stayed home until the police were able to clear the road again.

Major news networks did not report in the Solomon Islands, so we just had to guess at what the news might be. The local radio would give a sentence or two sometimes, but we never got the in-depth reporting we really wanted. We couldn't go to the beach, and I no longer felt safe walking alone in town. Libby was in the market with another family when a riot broke out, and the ladies selling produce grabbed the kids to hide them under tables. For 18 months, we lived in uncertainty, never knowing what was really going on. At night, we listened to the neighborhood noises and wondered if people were having a party, or if a rioting mob was headed our way.

The coup

Honiara, June 2000

One Monday morning we woke up and heard on the radio that the MEF had pulled off a coup. In a coordinated effort, they had broken into a bunch of police armories, and gained control of all the major weapons in the country.

This sounded scary, but it was eerily peaceful. The GRA had melted away into the jungle, since their homemade guns and bows and arrows were no match for the military-grade weaponry the MEF now commanded.

The next morning, I woke up early and heard a rumbling series of booms, a staccato thunder, off toward the airport. It went on and on. I called the police and described the sound. I asked them what was going on. They said, "Oh, we don't know. We are just neutral now." I called the Australian High Commission (the Australian embassy) and described the sound. I repeated my earlier question: "What is that noise? What's going on?" They didn't know either. Later on we found out that the MEF had taken the country's one gunboat, and were shelling the oil palm plantations by the airport where they suspected the GRA were hiding.

Our organization's regional director called me from his home in Brisbane, Australia to see how we were holding up.

"I'm pretty nervous," I remember saying to him.

"What about Andy? How's he doing?" our perceptive boss pursued.

"He's so calm I have to check him for a pulse every now and then," I said.

Even though we were now on much better terms with each other, we still had wildly divergent responses to crises. I saw everything as a threat to my kids' safety and my own ability to cope, while Andy saw exciting problems to solve and more worlds to conquer. Although I admired how he faced up to things, I just couldn't get myself to do the same. I felt better about myself, more confident in God's love, but mostly it still seemed like I wasn't competent and capable enough for everything I was supposed to be doing. I didn't know how to get past that.

That Thursday, I was listening to the radio news at 4:30 in the afternoon. At the end of the broadcast, they announced that women and children from Commonwealth countries (like Australia and New Zealand) were required to go to the yacht club at 5:00, a mere 30 minutes later, to be evacuated from the Solomon Islands on the Australian military transport ship, *Tobruk*. Just that one sentence. That was it.

Andy was at the office, doing the daily radio sked with families out in their villages. I called him to tell him what I had heard on the news. We had Commonwealth families in our group, so obviously they needed to go, but what about the American families?

What was going on, really? Had things suddenly gotten worse? What did the Australians know that we didn't know? Quickly, Andy phoned our regional director in Australia, and they decided that everyone who could go, should go.

Then at 4:45, the American embassy liaison officer called me and said that American women and children should also be at the yacht club by 5:00 for evacuation. The liaison officer told me that the US and Australia had a reciprocal agreement for situations like this. If Australia deemed an evacuation necessary, they would provide passage for US citizens as well as their own. The US would do the same for Australians whenever needed. However, the officer said, once the evacuation was done, it was done. If US citizens chose to ignore Australia's kind offer, the US government wouldn't come back after us. This was the only offer we were going to get. Take it or leave it.

I was ready to take it, no questions asked. Having grown up overseas, and having heard countless stories of missionary families being evacuated from war zones, I had packed our bags on Monday morning when we first heard about the coup. I had two carry-on-sized duffle bags, packed with a few changes of clothing for each of us, and all our photo albums.

The kids each had their own little back pack with whatever they'd chosen to bring. After the vagaries of ship travel in the Solomons, they'd had plenty of practice in how to pick up their favorite things and go at a moments' notice. Libby had her mini-me doll, Emily. Matt had his illustrated book of World History, which he had completely memorized, photo captions included. Michael had a long-eared bunny, and Jacob had a no-spill plastic bubble jar he always wanted with him. Unfortunately, nobody thought to bring the Legos. We certainly wished for them later on.

We knew that Andy had to stay in Honiara, because there were several families in the outer islands who could not be immediately evacuated on *Tobruk*. They would come in to town as they could, to be evacuated by plane. The plan, as we knew it, was for *Tobruk* to take the bulk of the expatriate community off the islands, and then the Australian government would send planes for those remaining.

I loaded the kids and our limited belongings into our van, leaving behind our cat and dog to join the packs of half-feral animals that always roamed the town. We stopped by the office to collect Andy, who was just finishing up the radio sked.

Andy drove us to the Yacht Club, where we waited until 10:00 that night, when the kids and I boarded a troop landing craft, just like the ones the Marines had used on Guadalcanal in World War 2. In our hurry to leave the house, we hadn't had dinner, or anything to drink. We were tired and scared and crying after saying goodbye to Andy. A Japanese businessman handed us a Coke, which I still consider one of the nicest gifts I have ever received.

We were on *Tobruk* for five days. Two of those days we waited in harbor for another ship to come as a safe haven for those still ashore, and three days we sailed in "moderate seas" to Cairns, Australia.

Tobruk is a huge tank-landing ship, flat-bottomed, designed to be pulled up onto a beach so that the tanks can be driven straight out onto the battlefield. The design is wonderful for tanks; however, it is not so fabulous for smaller persons tumbling around in its depths while underway in "moderate seas."

We slept in the tank crew quarters: long rooms with bunks stacked three-high along each wall. There were 45 people in our room, and 38 of them were under age 10. Each bunk had a seatbelt so that you could strap yourself in at night and not be thrown out onto the steel floor. The first night, while we were still in harbor, someone's kid rolled out of bed and broke his nose.

The bunks were stacked so closely that even Jacob, at 3 years old, couldn't sit up. Not that he wanted to sit up anyway. He was so traumatized by leaving his dog and his daddy behind, that he wouldn't leave my side. He stayed in bed with me for the entire trip. Libby, Matt, and Michael, however, had a fine time running all over the ship with their friends. If you ask them about it today, they will tell you that it was a five-day sleepover party with all their friends and endless Pringles. They also fondly recall the little individual boxes of cereal, the piles of apples, and the Gatorade they hadn't seen in three years.

Given my troubled relationship with ocean-going vessels, it was no surprise that I was seasick almost the whole time. The ship's crew came around regularly with seasickness tablets, which did keep me from throwing up, but made me so sleepy I could barely move.

The ship's fresh-water ballast tank was situated directly under my section of the cabin. When the ship started rolling, water whooshed across the tank and crashed into the opposite wall, right underneath me. The steel tiles of the floor creaked and gave, and a giant steel cabinet at the foot of my bed leaped off the floor, slamming back down with every wave. Whereas my older children can hardly remember having more fun, the trip for me was a drugged haze of crashing, rolling steel and water, a traumatized toddler, and worrying about my husband back in the Solomon Islands.

With hundreds of people aboard and limited phone capacity, the crew could only arrange one ship-to-shore phone call per person during the voyage. When my turn came, I tried to call Andy but couldn't get through. I then called our boss's wife in Australia, and she said that she thought he had gotten on a flight earlier that day, bound for Australia. When we arrived in Cairns, though, Andy was still in Honiara, and I just about lost it. I had not been in great shape when I got on the ship, and then I hadn't really slept in five days. My friend, Roxanne, went to one of our Australian administrators, who had flown in to help with logistics, and said, "You really need to get Andy here, because Kay's not doing well."

He immediately called Andy in Honiara. While they were on the phone, Andy looked up and saw a plane coming in. He had been keeping a packed bag with him in the office, so he grabbed his bag and went to the airport. He arrived in Cairns just 12 hours after we did, which made me wish we had all waited for the plane. We spent 5 days in Cairns, sorting out travel arrangements, and then flew back to the United States.

We went back to Tennessee, where we had spent our first furlough. I said to my sister, "I feel like I had a very bad dream, and then I woke up in Wal-Mart." It was hard to put the pieces back together again, and I noticed I was having a hard time making decisions. I was tired all the time and didn't have much energy for doing extra things.

One of my dear friends, Annie, would come over and walk with me almost every day. We used to walk past this little white church that had a cemetery on the hill above it. They had one of those signs outside where they'd put up pithy sayings. At one point the sign said, "Jesus is the friend who knows all about you and loves you anyway." As our route took us past that sign, day after day, it started to bother me. Finally one morning I said to Annie, "I think the thing that bothers me is the 'anyway.' I think it should be: 'Jesus is the friend who knows all about you and loves you.' I think He loves us without the anyway."

Andy kept working on the translation project while we were in Tennessee, and he drove a dump truck for a construction crew to bring in some extra money. Our salary from supporters was adequate for a third-world country, but not very livable in America. Then one month, a bookkeeper in our organization did something backwards which resulted in our salary being subtracted from our account, instead of added to it. Apparently, however, the mistake couldn't be rectified until the following month, which was difficult indeed.

After 6 months in the States, we were on a plane again, headed back overseas. I was still very tired, not ready to go back, but our allotted time away from the Solomons was up, and financially, it was pretty stressful to stay in the States any longer. Things were still not great in the Solomon Islands, so we went instead to coastal Papua New Guinea, to be on staff at the orientation course we'd attended seven years earlier in 1993.

That year turned out to be one of the best years of our entire career overseas. Andy and I taught classes together, and worked closely with other staffers, while the kids attended a one-room school, which they adored. We helped new families make sense of what was going on as they transitioned into this extraordinary new life. I got to do things I enjoyed, that were valued. Just hanging out with people was a part of my job description. I was even asked to arrange flowers for meetings.

Since we were on staff and already knew how to do village life, we could relax and enjoy ourselves on weekends, rather than struggling to cook over an open fire. We took our kids down to the little resort at the beach on Sunday afternoons for fish and chips and a swim. *Survivor: Vanuatu* was on the one station our borrowed TV received, and we loved to watch other people struggle to make it in the South Pacific jungle. One memorable evening, we laughed ourselves silly as a cast member stood in a cassava garden and said, "There's nothing to eat here! We're doing to starve to death!" I'd had that feeling myself many times.

One of my favorite experiences of that year was a hike that Andy and I took, with three local guides. Our leader was Papa Damo, a man who delighted in maintaining traditional culture, and in teaching all of us about the real Papua New Guinea. He loved to dress in his customary regalia of a beaten-bark loincloth, a bone through his pierced nose, and a feather headdress waving fearsomely above it all. He almost always carried a bow and quiver of arrows with him, which tended to freak the newbies out a bit, until they got to know him.

He was dressed in modern shorts, but still carrying his bow and arrow, as we set off at first light, carrying light packs of food and water. As we descended into an area of virgin rain forest that had never been cut for gardens or timber, Papa Damo kept a sharp eye on the tree tops. Early in the morning, birds of paradise would come to feed in the rain forest canopy, and he was determined to find a flock for us. Soon enough, he sighted a group of birds, white and yellow and black and gold. As we stood under the trees and watched, it was like morning in the Garden of Eden: the hushed green of the rainforest, the gold of the sun just coming up, and the birds with their long, flowing tail feathers, resting and chattering in the tops of the trees.

That whole year was a time of rest for my soul. God led me to the story of prophet Elijah, under the broom tree, in I Kings 19. Here was Elijah, the prophet of God, who had worked so hard that he finally fell in his tracks and crawled under a tree, ready to die. God's response was to send an angel to touch Elijah, and to feed him, and to get him ready for the journey ahead.

I knew that part of the story. For the first time, though, I noticed that the angel fed Elijah twice, touched him twice, and that Elijah slept twice before getting up and going on. Those things assured me that it was okay for me to rest, and to rest in abundance. Initially, we had thought we would stay in PNG for 6 months, but at the end of those 6 months, we decided to stay longer, doing things we loved, and enjoying the journey. We ended up staying a full year.

Eventually, though, it was time to go back to the Solomons for at least one more year of village work, in order to finish up the Arosi New Testament translation. I felt pretty good about going back to village life again. It seemed like God had healed me in some major ways, and our marriage was a much happier place to be. We'd had this great year of doing things together and resting in work that fit. I knew that the project was almost done, and I went back to the Solomons with a renewed sense of purpose and peace about how to be okay with the daily realities of life.

Part 2

Journals from the year of endings

In January 2002, we were back in the Solomons, and back into the old routine of 3-month village stays, interspersed with brief town visits to restock for another village stay. Andy was concentrating on finishing the Arosi translation project, so he passed along his deputy director role to someone else. For the first time, we had a satellite phone in the village. Twice a week, we could send and receive email, if we pointed our little screen at exactly the right place in the sky. As a result of those emails, and the journal I kept that year, I have a close record of our last year of work in the Solomon Islands, the year of endings.

January 18, 2002—Honiara

What is the most dreaded sound for a missionary?
The howling of angry natives in the night?
The snapping of hungry crocodiles' jaws?
The rattle of machine-gun fire in the neighborhood?
Actually the most dreaded sound for the missionary would be the sound of packing tape ripping off the roll. It's been reverberating around our house most of the time in the past few days.

Tuesday night we thought that we might be going to the village on Wednesday afternoon. This provoked a veritable packing-tape frenzy. At the end of two hours of packing mania, Andy looked at me and said, "This is crazy. There's no way we can be ready by noon tomorrow." And then it turned out that that ship didn't go anyway. But hey, it sure got our packing kick-started.

Now it looks like we'll be going tomorrow (Saturday) afternoon, about 4 p.m., on a ship called the *Bulawa*. The *Bulawa* is, unfortunately, taking the scenic route—24 hours instead of 14. We get to tour the "weather coast" of our island, before turning back to take another look at it, then finally cruising around to our side of the island. The last time we toured the "weather coast", we found out that there was really a good reason they'd called it that. I didn't see a lot of the scenery, mostly concentrating on the inside of my eyelids or on the water directly below the railing. The good news this time is that this is cyclone season. In between cyclones, the sea is very fine. We're in between, so maybe this time around I'll actually enjoy it a bit more. Also we are trying a new seasickness remedy, Vicks in the belly-button. We've heard this works, and we're out to give it the acid test.

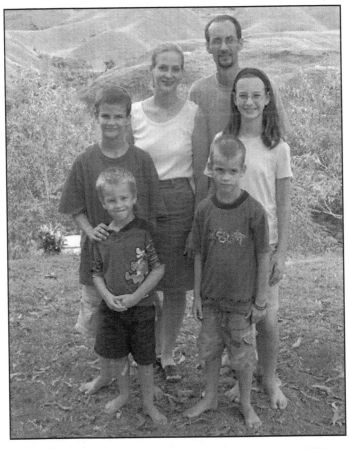

Family portrait, Honiara, Solomon Islands, January 2002

I don't know what kind of reception we will get in the village. We last visited as a family in December 1999. A few months after that visit, we were evacuated from the country after a coup. Now here we are again. I wonder what they will think of our return. The community is so tight-knit, all families and clans—is there a place for us again? How will my kids be in the village, after so long away?

January 20—Tawatana

The Vicks in the belly-button was an unqualified disaster. In fairness to the Vicks corporation, I have to admit that we bought the store brand rather than real Vicks. Maybe the cheap stuff is missing some vital ingredient. Maybe. The whole thing probably needs more serious testing, but I won't be volunteering. Next time, I'll just be taking Dramamine right off the bat.

Once we arrived in the village, though, everything was great. As soon as the kids on shore saw us climbing down into the dinghy, they ran into the water and swam out to meet us— all screaming, waving, and shooting water with bamboo water guns. "Mom," said Libby, "I feel like a celebrity." When we got to shore, the adults waded out to hold the dinghy steady, to lift the kids out, to shake hands, to carry the luggage, to laugh and greet us. Our front yard had been weeded and cleared, our door was open, and some young girls had been in to sweep and mop and wash the horizontal glass louvers. They had even washed the curtains. And we'd only been in the house about ten minutes when a steady stream of food began arriving at our door—bananas, pineapples, sweet potato soup.

Welcome home.

February 14—Honiara

We arrived back in Honiara, not according to plan. We had to come to town to finalize the sale of our Honiara house and to try to get the money out of the country before the falling Solomon dollar robs us of any more of the proceeds. The last time I saw my house was the day we got evacuated from it, June 8, 2000. I had fifteen minutes' notice to leave it. Andy has taken the kids back, but I've never gone. Too much loss; just let it go. So here we are to seal the deal.

Leaving the village by night was pretty spectacular. It was pitch black, overcast and raining lightly. We waited at a house near the beach, and the lady of the house had just opened her stone oven. She served us the most fantastic sweet potato baked with gallons of coconut cream. When the cry came that the ship was coming, we grabbed our luggage, stumbling through the dark, wading across the creek, bumbling through the sand. The ship slowed down and turned in toward the village—always a relief, because we're never 100% sure that it's going to stop for us, until it actually does. The ship's dinghy buzzed toward us like a crazed hornet, reversed, and floated ashore on a wave. The rain stopped and some boys lit a bonfire of coconut leaves down the beach a ways, right at the edge of the water. They were dancing around it like a bunch of wild cannibals, which their great-grandfathers certainly were. We got into the dinghy and headed out for the ship. Everything was pitch black, and Jake was scared until we noticed the phosphorescence being churned up beside the dinghy. Fire in the water, fire on the beach.

When we got to the ship, we had to climb about 8 feet up a ladder, from a bobbing dinghy onto a rolling ship. Nine years since the first time we did this, it still makes me nervous to see my precious little babies swarming up the side of the ship like monkeys. I just had to watch, which meant that I lost sight of the horizon and so, just as soon as I crawled up the ladder and got my feet on deck, I lost all that wonderful sweet potato, back into the water.

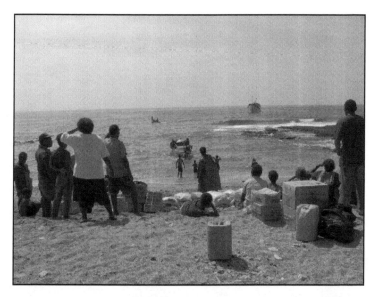

February 16—Honiara

I found a lump in my right breast. I examine my breasts every month, always feeling kind of sheepish, like I'm some kind of paranoid alarmist. I can't believe this. I keep feeling it again and again, to make sure that I haven't imagined it. I'm not even turning 36 for four more days. This can't be real.

February 18—Honiara

I went to the doctor this morning, Dr. Kori. The waiting room is noisy and crowded with people having malaria slides done. You can tell they're having slides because they are all gripping hunks of cotton balls, after having their fingers stabbed. Not too many people actually go in to see the doctor; they just find out if their slide is positive and buy the medicine they need. So I get in to see the doctor without much of a wait. He feels the lump and says that I can't get a mammogram done here. I have to go to Australia.

February 20—Honiara

It's my birthday. We finalized the sale of our house and I have a lump in my breast. I doubt I will forget this one.

The ladies had a birthday tea for me at Martha's house. Beth made me the cutest sunflower cake and everybody brought me a gift. It helped make a weird day a lot better.

We also went out for dinner at the nicest restaurant in Honiara. It was their buffet night, with the price four times its usual. Since it had been 18 months since we'd been out for dinner alone, we decided to go for it anyway.

February 28—Brisbane, Australia

I went to the breast clinic today. It was the most amazing place. There were NO MEN working there. There were half a dozen ladies wearing nametags labeled "volunteer". One of these ladies took me into the changing room, gave me a hanger for my clothes and a snazzy pale green kimono. Andy got to sit in a small lounge room for the "partners"—the only place that men were allowed to be. They had a whole separate waiting room for women only.

I got my first mammogram and really it's the only time in my life I've been glad to be small-breasted. It reminded me of making chicken Kiev, putting the chicken between sheets of plastic wrap and smashing it flat.

I also saw a doctor and she said that I've got a blocked duct, and it's no big deal, it will go away. Good news. The best news. I felt guilty, looking around the room and knowing that a lot of those women wouldn't get good news.

March 3—Brisbane

We're spending the weekend at a hotel in The City as they call downtown here. Walking to parks, museums, shopping; seeing movies, eating out. We got a bottle of wine and had a picnic in the park. Loved just being together by ourselves, happy and at peace.

One time some friends of ours, working in the Solomons, went home to Australia for a few months. The first time they took their kids to a mall, their daughter ran around screaming, "I'm in heaven! I'm in heaven!"

That's pretty much what it feels like.

March 5—Honiara

Honiara again. Reality bites. Our director asked Andy if we would stay on here after Christmas, and take on the deputy director job again. I cried when he told me. Andy says we don't have to do it; we just need to think about it. We were planning to go to Papua New Guinea, where there's a big missionary center, so the kids could go to a real school while Andy finishes the last bits of the New Testament before we publish it. Home schooling for me is a daily reminder of my incompetence—and I've had nine years of that; I've been counting on getting the kids into a real school after Christmas. But Andy likes the deputy job; and he could probably get all the translation work finished by mid-year if we stayed here in the Solomons. I think we will stay. I can't stop crying.

March 10—Tawatana

We saw the most amazing things from the ship this time. First, we sailed through a school of thousands of pink jellyfish, ranging in color from pale rose to wild fuschia. Some were the size of a fist, others like turkey platters. They all squeezed shut and burst open again, and their tentacles hung like curtains from orange circles on their undersides. The captain of the ship said that a deep-sea current comes up at that particular spot and the jellyfish ride to the surface with the current. We must have sailed through the jellyfish for ten minutes.

Then the sun went down behind the boat and the whole sky and sea became one pure sheet of orange. Just as the sun went down, a light rain began to fall and in front of the ship was a huge rainbow. We sailed right toward the center of the rainbow.

March 12—*Tawatana*

One of the things I bought in Brisbane is a new book by Henri Nouwen, called *Turn My Mourning into Dancing*. He talks about life as the movement between all the different aspects of life, happy and sad, joyful and painful.

Reading this book gave me permission to realize that the past couple of years have been a time of loss for me in a lot of areas. We've gained some of the things back; we made it back here, and it looks like we'll be able to finish the New Testament. But there were serious casualties of the evacuation—friends who didn't return or ended up leaving because of the changes in the country. There were incidental losses—things that just disappeared from our house after we left the country—including all my shoes, some of my favorite clothes, and the Georgia O'Keefe Sunflowers poster my friend Pam gave me. These things were mine, taken from me without my permission.

Our friends Pat and Beth are going in a few weeks, finishing their project—that will be a major loss for me and for the rest of our family too. All the changes in the group—it's such a different place now, and that is a nebulous kind of loss, but still a loss.

Just finishing up the village work and planning a move ourselves also represents a loss. I'm trying to grieve when I'm sad. At the same time, I have to keep living. Sometimes I want to just break down and bawl for days, but I have to keep cooking, hanging up the laundry, teaching school. It's hard to find a time and place to grieve.

Good Friday/Easter—*Tawatana*

On Friday the community did the 14 Stations of the Cross. It's a mobile pageant that goes all over the village; at each station, there's somebody playing the part of a disciple, Simon of Cyrene, Mary, or Pontius Pilate. They give their thoughts, and everybody else walks along and sings hymns. I was doing the two stations of toilet and bed that day, so I didn't go. Andy had a part as one of the disciples, so he did the whole thing and so did Libby. The boys joined up about halfway through, when it went past our house. I think they really did get something out of it, as Jake was pretty upset when they "nailed" Jesus to the cross. Sunday was a communion service, which takes a long time because they sing the whole liturgy and everybody goes to the front to receive Communion. I like it, now that I'm more used to it. The musical setting for the communion liturgy is really beautiful. It helps that the kids are older now, too. They just know that they have to sit there. When Michael was little, he figured that everybody had come to church to look at him (which was pretty much the case). He was such a terrible ham at church that I quit taking him at all.

After church we had another feast followed by "entertainment". I say "entertainment" because it doesn't entertain us all that much. Somehow, we really miss the boat when it comes to their sense of humor. There's some body of knowledge that is a closed book to us. The funniest thing to us was a whole group of ladies, our close neighbors and leaders of the church women's group, who dressed up in men's clothes (women here usually DO NOT wear pants), including sunglasses, boots, and construction helmets. They looked hilarious. But then came the inscrutable part. They pretended to be paddling a canoe to Malaita. Everyone was roaring with laughter and we were mystified. Why was it funny to paddle a canoe to Malaita? Go figure. I feel like the longer I live here, the less I understand.

April 2—Tawatana

I think we've adopted contingency-style school as our permanent operating basis. So far this year the kids are getting the bare bones. Maybe we will be able to settle better the next time we are out in the village. It's just been really hard to get into anything for the last couple of months—too much moving around. The uncertainty in the country constantly hangs in the background. The last time we went to Honiara, we were unpacking our "town stuff" when we heard gunfire from the direction of the main road. It's just always there.

Most days I'm really encouraged about Michael's reading progress and start to hope for a certain level of independence before long which would make it easier to give more attention to the older ones. Libby and Matt are just on their own most of the time with their text books, and I don't like that. This morning was kind of a disaster, who knows why.

Michael is such an imaginative child, full of energy and enthusiasm for life. When he was little, he would always say he was going on "abentures." He's the one who will bring me flowers and tell me he loves me. But when it comes to school, he just gets in a funk some days and can't seem to think. At those times I just don't push it. I know from long experience that it just makes him worse. I don't know if I'm getting smarter or just getting tired-er.

I'm kind of in a funk myself if the truth were to be told. Combination of things, I guess. Had a cold and lost my voice this week—that's probably the most immediate trigger.

Beth leaves in two weeks—that leaves me feeling like my last friend has abandoned me. I hate the thought of going to town and not having anybody to really talk to—after being in the village for months without anybody to really talk to. I feel like I have to be tough for Andy and not burden him with my uncomfortable emotions while he's pushing so hard to get done. I'm still upset at having to stay on here past Christmas; I had set myself a year as the time I had to deal with here. Then to find out that we have to stay on for another six months and take the deputy job again for part of that . . . I just don't really know how to deal with it.

I've been re-reading the Henri Nouwen book *Can You Drink the Cup?* He talks about being grateful for all the things that have gone into our lives to bring us to where we are—not just the good stuff. I find it's possible to do that with distance and time, but I find it so hard to be thankful when I'm going through a time like this. It's not disastrous, just uncomfortable and no relief on the horizon.

April 18—Honiara

We survived another ocean voyage. It still surprises me when we arrive in one piece and basically in our right minds. It seems like the sort of experience that should kill you or send you to the nearest loony bin.

We had a private cabin this time, which means extra space and some privacy. We have four separate bunks in the cabin, and when we sleep on deck, we have two little mattresses. The extra space, however, comes with extra passengers of the insect variety, because the private cabin hosts the ship's enormous and voracious cockroach population. We try to keep them at bay by spraying down the entire cabin with insecticide as soon as we board the ship, and this tends to keep things civilized for a while. In the dead of night, in the dark, though, the bug spray always wears off and then we'll be awakened to the tickling of little feet and tentacles all over our bodies.

And then there's the ship's toilet. The toilet room is about 2 feet wide, and the doorknob sometimes does not lock very well. It adds excitement to the event, not knowing if the door is going to pop open at a strategic moment. I always hang on to the knob for privacy's sake.

Another interesting thing about the ship's toilet is the liquid on the floor. I try not to think about that too much, just be charitable and assume that some nice clean water sloshed out at some point. Oh, and there's no TP, so you have to bring your own along.

So this morning, there I was, hanging on to the door with one hand and my roll of TP with the other, soggy at the ankles and trying to hold my skirt up out of the "water". I had a fresh tampon gripped between my teeth like a flamenco dancer nibbles a rose, wondering what I would let go of in order to proceed. All I could think was, "How in the heck did I ever get here?" I mean, what series of bizarre events led me, a somewhat normal American person, into the toilet of the *MV Kaona*?

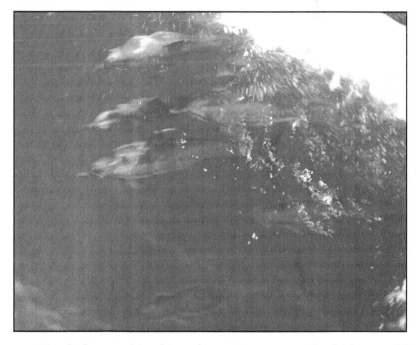

To balance this bit of nastiness, we had Seaworld Solomons. A pod of dolphins came alongside the bow of the ship and swam with us for ages. They were just cruising along, hardly moving a muscle, it seemed. Just out for a stroll. Leaping and spinning whenever they felt like it. All of a sudden, they'd had enough of us, and took off for open water.

Thinking back on all the ship travel I've endured here, it seems the experiences fall into those two extremes: the sublime and the horrific. I think I will look back on the whole Solomons experience that way. There have been times of sublime happiness and times of horrific pain. It's just life. Weird, but life.

April 21—Honiara

Well, it's been an exhausting day emotionally. We saw Pat and Beth off at the airport this morning. It's hard to believe that our nine years of being family together here in the Solomons is over. It just doesn't seem real that they are finished with their project and gone. I didn't actually cry too much at the airport, mostly just got teary and couldn't talk. I even smiled at Beth as she was going through that horrible door that swallows all my friends. Then we came home and I went straight to my bedroom and lay under the ceiling fan and bawled for about an hour. The kids kept coming in and looking at me. Andy sat with me, turned on the AC (this is the only house with AC in one of the rooms), listened to me, brought me a Coke with lots of ice, and generally acted like Super Husband.

We decided that we will definitely be going to Ukarumpa at the end of this year, and not doing the deputy director job again. I just have no emotional energy for that. I can get excited about the village and how things are going there; I can hold it together in Tawatana for the sake of the translation, but when it comes to thinking of doing admin again, and another complete year of home schooling, I get totally depressed. This last month in the village has been so hard, thinking all the time "I have to be all things to all men for another year or more."

No matter how much I think the translation is worth it, the thought of doing admin again was just hanging over me like a huge cloud. So today we talked about all that and Andy finally convinced me that it's okay to not feel responsible for the entire group, and just do what we think is best for us (including me). He can get a lot of the checking done by email, plus make a couple of trips back from PNG when he needs to. So that is the latest plan. I feel like I can make it now. Super Husband saves the day.

I think it's just been a long haul for me, nine years of doing things that I don't feel very good at, and which consequently exhaust me, especially home schooling.

I said to Beth the other day, I just need some help (practical help, not psychiatric care, although some days that seems like a good idea, too). I feel like I just have to hold it together by myself in so many areas: spiritually (without church or fellowship in my language), physically (without medical care), emotionally (with friends leaving)—and I have to hold it together for my kids, too, trying to provide all that they would get from school, Sunday School, extracurricular activities—and feeling guilty when I can't. Plus trying to keep track of all their emotional issues and be the family therapist. I don't think there's really much that can be done to change this, it's just the name of the game, but it's exhausting long-term when I don't get a break from it at all. The political situation here is just the icing on the cake. Things are still not great after the coup. It still doesn't feel safe. I'm pretty much at the end of my resources, and it's time to call up the reserves in the form of the Ukarumpa International Primary School.

There's an old story about a guy caught in a flood. As the waters rose, he climbed out onto the roof of his house and prayed that God would save him. Pretty soon a neighbor came by in a canoe. "Hop in," says the neighbor. "No," says the guy, "God is going to save me." After a while another friend comes by in a motorboat. "Get in," says the friend. "No," says the guy, "God is going to save me." Well, the water is creeping up around his neck when a rescue helicopter flies up and a frogman jumps into the water. "Grab on," says the frogman. "No way," says the guy. "God is going to save me." Sure enough, the guy drowns and when he gets to heaven, right away he confronts the Lord. "I prayed and prayed. Why didn't you save me?" he demands. "Mister," says the Lord, "Three times I tried."

I have the feeling that I just got into the motorboat.

May 10—Honiara

I'm having another medical situation that's making me nervous. I'm having some weird vaginal discharge. Three days last week I had this (in the middle of my cycle and I'm the world's most regular person). Then last night after an enjoyable interlude, if you know what I mean, it happened again. So I looked in the *1250 Healthcare Questions Women Ask* book (which I think I should just steal from the group library, since I seem to be using it all the time anyway) and at first I couldn't find anything that really described what I was having. Then finally I ran across this entry that talked about precancerous and cancerous conditions and it sounded just like what I've been having.

So I talked to my friend Virginia, who is a nurse, and she told me not to panic. It could just be a cyst or something, but I have to admit that I am kind of losing my sense of humor for these situations. Tomorrow (Saturday) I'm going in to Doctor Kori for a pap smear. Now isn't that a nice restful thing to look forward to for the weekend? He says that they will courier the slide to Australia, rather than sending it through the hospital system, so I figure that direct route is worth quite a bit of humiliation. A couple of other ladies tried a different clinic and never got results back, so I'm definitely not going to even try there, even though I would rather go to a different doctor for this. It was bad enough baring my breasts to him in February.

May 11—Honiara

It was another one of those memorable Solomons experiences. The best I can say is, it's done. The low point was when the speculum got stuck, open, internally, and the doc's gloves were too lubricated to get any traction to unstick it. He took two slides and gave them to me. I will pass them on to a colleague who is going to Brisbane on Tuesday and he will pass them on to our office staff who will take them to the lab . . . and so we have by-passed the hospital here, and should get a result back within two weeks.

It also turns out that I have a polyp on the cervix. Hopefully it's just a benign thing. But still, I don't want to live with this bleeding long-term and I need to have the polyp removed. How to do that here is another story. Supposedly it's not that complicated—but in a country where the hospital doesn't have syringes . . . and where they will splint your arm with a piece torn from a cardboard box . . .

May 13—Honiara

Well, I think I'm closer to hysteria this morning than I've been in my life. All I want is to get this stupid little cervical polyp removed. According to the book and medical advice from the civilized world, this should be a matter of a decent doctor, a speculum, a ring clamp, and a simple twisting motion. How hard can that be, right? In fact it sounds like I could do it myself if I had eyes in the right part of my body.

The polyp should also be sent to Australia for routine pathology. There's a flight tomorrow. This is the day.

So my first step toward assembling the proper components for polyp removal was a phone call to my friend, Virginia, the nurse. She says she will do the twisting if I can find the instruments. So I call Doctor Kori; he reiterates that he does not want to do it; it's beyond his area of experience. So I say that Virginia will come along and do the deed. He perks up immediately, but then I mention the words "ring clamp" and that's the end of that. He suggests that I call the Fema Clinic and see if Doctor Quan is still working there, because Quan is a gynecologist.

So we look in the phone book but no sign of Fema Clinic in the "F" pages. Look in the yellow pages under "medical", "clinic", "doctor" and "physician". No dice. Can't think of any other arcane words describing medical facilities. Call directory assistance. No answer. Call Doctor Kori's office. Ask them for the number. They don't know either. Finally have the brainwave of looking for a home number. Phone Doctor Quan's home. No, Quan is not at the clinic. He's working at his store, LOS Trading.

I call LOS Trading. Doctor Quan apologizes but he is not doing any clinical work this year. (Neither was he doing clinical work in 1994, when Michael was born, so I think the Chinese store must be more lucrative than the clinic.) Quan tells me that I will need to go to the hospital, land of no syringes and cardboard-box arm splints. He says they will give me a general anesthetic "because of the instruments they have". (What does he mean, some kind of medieval torture instruments?) He says that I need to call the hospital, see if the gynecology clinic is still operating, and see if Doctor Zutu is still working there, or if they can get Doctor Zutu to come in for this procedure. (Presumably I should also check and see if they still have ring clamps and a speculum.) I barely thank him. I hang up and start shrieking and banging my head on the wall. I can't even tell Andy what he's said. I run to my room and cry hysterically. The kids are all convinced that I'm totally losing my mind. I am too.

Andy gets back on the phone with Doctor Quan and tries to find out why I need a general anesthesia for this simple procedure. Turns out Doctor Quan thinks I should have a D & C as well as the polyp removal. But when Andy makes it clear that we don't want a D & C, we just want the polyp off, Quan says that Doctor Zutu should be able to do the twist. Not trusting the hospital's phone system to actually be able to make contact with Doctor Zutu, Andy takes off to see what he can find out.

If we fall at this fence, the polyp will go to Brisbane, attached to my body. It seems bizarre that I would have to go to Australia for something so simple, but somehow it seems we've fallen through the looking glass into a strange world where the simplest things are incredibly complex.

May 21—Honiara

I had another interesting visit to the doctor. This is Doctor Zutu, the reported gynecologist. He works at the hospital but also has office hours at another clinic where I can make an appointment. If I go to the hospital, I will wait in line indefinitely. So I make the clinic appointment. The first thing I notice about the examining room is the lack of that big bright light that gynecologists always have at the foot of the bed. Hmm. Next observation is that Doctor Zutu looks pretty young. And seems a little nervous, or perhaps has ADHD since he seems to have a hard time sitting still. So we have a little chat about my symptoms, then the exam begins.

The nurse comes in with the speculum. Then there's a question of lubrication for the speculum. The nurse pulls a lidless tube of something from a cardboard box. The doctor doesn't like that one. She tosses it back in the box. She goes out and comes back with a 1-liter bottle of sonogram jelly—also lidless. He rejects that one, too. They mention KY, but it appears to be unavailable. So they revert to lidless tube #1 and use that. Once the speculum is inserted, they start talking about a flashlight. Aha, they have also noticed that the big bright light is missing. Discussion on flashlight reveals that somebody took the flashlight somewhere and they don't have one anymore. This office is right next to a Chinese store that sells everything from tuna fish to flip-flops, and probably even flashlights. But no one thinks of solving the problem that way, apparently.

So the exam proceeds. Finally it's over and THEN he tells me that I will need to come down to the hospital during his clinic there on Thursday, where they have a light.

He tells me that he did feel something on the cervix, but he thinks that there is also something going on with the uterus. The uterus is not spongy; it's hard. And I can testify that it is quite painful when pressed. He says something about possible fibroids and then he starts talking about general anesthetic. He wants me to go in tomorrow for a sonogram; then to his clinic at the hospital on Thursday for another exam; then to the hospital on Friday for a D&C.

I don't think so. I think I would rather spend my time and energy getting a medical visa for Australia. I'll have to go by myself since Andy is stuck behind the director's desk for the next month. I'm not real excited about going to Australia by myself, but it genuinely scares me to have anything done at the hospital. I mean, if I need to bring my own KY and flashlight to the private clinic, there's no telling what might happen if I'm under general anesthesia at the public hospital.

June 3—Honiara

Our ceiling is raining maggots.

Yesterday morning I was sweeping the floor and found all these little grub-looking things, crawling from behind the couch, toward the kitchen. Disgusto. So I swept them all up, and a few minutes later I found a few more in the middle of the living room floor, headed toward the kitchen. We all started looking around for the source of these grubs, and finally Andy realized that they were dropping from the molding between the wall and the ceiling, behind the couch. Then they start heading like lemmings for the kitchen. He shot a bunch of bug spray into the molding, but the grubs kept dropping. We commented on how they really looked like maggots, but how could a house have maggots?

So last night after Brazil beat Turkey in World Cup soccer, and the neighbors quieted down enough that we could have a conversation, we started talking about these grubs again. Then we connected this funny gas-like smell that I've been noticing in the living room with these grubs. Eeeyew, there must be a dead rat in the attic. DOUBLE DISGUSTO, they really ARE maggots!!!!

Why are they dropping down into our living room and heading for the kitchen? We aren't quite sure, but it doesn't speak well for my cooking.

June 6—Brisbane

Back in Australia again. I went to the gynecologist yesterday and had a totally painless pelvic exam. She removed the polyp without my even knowing it. This morning I went to a diagnostic clinic for a couple of ultrasounds. The doctor there says that I have "thickening of the myometrium consistent with adenomyosis." What I understand is that the lining of my uterus is growing "roots" down into the muscle. Causes a painful uterus and funny bleeding. It's benign, just annoying, and my case is mild so there is no treatment at present.

June 8—Brisbane

I'm totally exhausted; spent the last two days in bed, hoping that I'm not getting malaria. But I think it's just that sick exhaustion from too much stress. I used to do this on Spring Break from college. Come home and get sick. It's winter here, so I haven't really minded staying tucked up in bed. It's wonderful to be cold and under the covers.

June 11—Honiara

When I got back here, Andy told me that he'd run into a Nigerian friend of ours, who's the head of pediatrics at the hospital. When Andy related some of the drama I had endured, Doctor Dan said, "Oh, no, she didn't go to Doctor Zutu! Not Doctor Zutu! That man's not a gynecologist!" Apparently they don't have an actual gynecologist right now; Doctor Zutu is just filling in until they recruit a real one. Can't be too soon, I say.

June 24—Honiara

I've been tangling with the health care profession again today, to my detriment. This time it's the dentist. When we were in the village in March, I broke a filling. When we first came into town, I was busy dealing with female issues and couldn't face the stress of the dentist on top of the BYO gynecologists. But now, with five months in the village ahead, I knew I had to get this tooth dealt with. So last Thursday, I went in thinking that it would be a half hour thing. But no, the dentist said I had to have a root canal.

This is the same guy that did a root canal on Andy's dad in 1997 without Novocain. But I've dealt with him before, so I know enough to beg for the drugs before the drilling begins. He's actually a good dentist, I think. Just doesn't see the need for anesthesia for some reason. But he does use it on me—because I ask him to. He always gives me a look like "Really? Why would you want such a thing?" He probably thinks I'm the biggest wimp on the planet, but it doesn't matter. I just want to be numb.

After three Novocain shots and an hour of excavation on Thursday, he said he had done all he could for one appointment, and wanted me to come back on Monday morning to finish digging, plaster up the hole, and call it a day.

So this morning, there I am in the chair, numb to the eyeballs, when the power goes off.

The power used to go off at regular times each day, (the power company preserving fuel) so the dentist could schedule appointments around the power outages. But in the past week, it's started going off at odd times. The dentist used to have a back-up generator, but that got stolen. He's sorry, but he doesn't know what to tell me. He rings the power company and they say that the electricity might come back on in a couple of hours. There are already three other people sitting in the waiting room, and I can see in the appointment book that more are scheduled to arrive. Waiting around doesn't seem like a good option. Other morning appointments are filled for the next few days, and he's not making afternoon appointments, because he's pretty sure the power will be off then.

I can't wait for another morning appointment, because we're supposed to be going to the village in a couple of days. If we miss that ship, it may be a couple of weeks before another one goes; we have a group of six college kids coming to our village around July 10. We've got to get to the village and finish making arrangements for their visit. I don't have time for this stupid tooth and the crazy power outages.

Finally I remember that our group owns a small, portable (if you're strong) generator. I think it might be enough to run the dental compressor and lights. So I ask if I could bring it along, and the dentist is most enthusiastic. So I reschedule for 3, me and my generator.

When I get back to the dentist at three, the power is still off, so we haul the generator out of the car. He gets it revved up outside, near a window, and runs an extension cord inside through a hole in the fly screen. He plugs in his equipment, and we go inside. He gives me a shot of Novocain and is just starting some more excavation of the jaw, when the generator starts to rev up and then slow down and rev up again. He goes outside to try to fix it and then his assistant and I notice this burning rubber smell. So we run to the window and tell him to shut it off, because something is burning. Investigation reveals a strip outlet, charred and blackened.

Obviously the generator isn't helping anything—in fact, it is doing damage, so we load it back in the car, and I sit down to wait to see if the regular power might come back on. After an hour's wait, it still isn't on, so I make another appointment for Wednesday morning and head home. Later Monday night, I start to think about all the equipment that had been plugged into the generator. What if some of the stuff wasn't on a surge protector? What if that strip outlet didn't have a surge protector? His computer, fridge, compressor, autoclave, lights . . . this could be the million-dollar root canal.

Andy finds an instruction book for the generator and in the fine print, sees a place where it says not to move the throttle switch, as the thing could put out upwards of 400 volts. We run on 240 here. There is no gauge anywhere on the generator to show that the voltage output could vary. The book says to run the generator at 1500-1900 rpms, but there is also no gauge for that. Maybe we are just supposed to be able to tell by the sound of the engine? Count the blades as they go by? I don't know. Needless to say, this is not a machine that we will ever be tempted to use again.

June 25—Honiara

This morning I was a nervous wreck, imagining all that I might have to pay for. Finally Andy calls up the dentist and asks how the equipment has fared. "Righty-ho" said the good dentist. Whew.

June 26—Honiara

This morning the power held up long enough to finish the digging and plastering. I sincerely hope that that is the last I will see of a dentist's chair for a very long time.

This whole root canal saga wasn't the most fun I've ever had. And I don't know that I took it all that calmly. The first day I went, when he spent an hour digging away, I just sat there and cried the whole time. It was pretty embarrassing, but I just couldn't help it. I just couldn't believe it was happening to me. I needed to cry, so I cried. The poor dentist. I don't know what he thought. I can't even plead PMS. I was just pitiful. Then we had the day that the generator blew up his surge protector, the day I went twice and got nothing but Novocain shots—that day when I came back, the first person I talked to was our friend Greg. He asked me how I was, and I started crying all over him, too. The next day, my legs were so sore I could barely walk. I realized that I had been so tense, sitting in that chair, that I made myself sore. So I haven't been a hero over this. I'm merely a survivor. I think next time I would rather let my teeth rot right out of my head. Or maybe I'll order a handy pair of ice skates, so I could just bash it out like Tom Hanks in *Castaway*.

I sent out emails to our friends about the root canal, and I got lots of responses. This one, from my sister-in-law's dad, was my favorite:

Dear Kay:

I am writing on behalf of your dentist - who called me last evening and asked me to help you plan for your next visit to him. He said that if you would bring your own chair it would help. And if Andy had an extra drill or two in his workshop and could send them along it might be wise. He also wants me to tell you to bring your own Novocain - and even better than bringing it with you – if you could give yourself the shots before you come, then you'd be ready for him to work on you and you could save some time. Please do this. He would also like you to bring an extra flashlight with you and practice holding it up so it shines into your mouth while he is working. There's a little shadow to one side and if you would train yourself to shine the light there he could be more certain of working on the correct tooth. Oh, and if you would bring a towel or a bib to wear it would help keep his costs down. He's a bit bashful about telling you these things and asked me if I would help. Thanks for your compliance with the new rules of our office.

Pastor Somers

alias Ruthless Toothless

June 27—Honiara

Andy called the shipping office this morning to see if we can get an idea of when we might be leaving for the village. The guy he talked to said that the ship should arrive back in Honiara Thursday. Then, he said, they usually like to be in Honiara for two days, and then take another trip (a pattern we have also observed). So, he said, he thought that they would be leaving on Tuesday. Hmm, says Andy, if they arrive on Thursday, then wouldn't two days be more like Saturday or Sunday? Wouldn't Tuesday be more like four or five days? Yes, says the guy, but I think they will go on Tuesday.

So maybe we'll be ready to go on Saturday, just in case, but expect to go on Tuesday? We'll keep calling to see if the story varies. At least we think that they are taking the direct, 16-hour route to the village as opposed to the scenic 24-hour route.

June 28—Honiara

Our friend Patteson, in town from the village, explains the shipping company's story to me. You see, he tells me, the World Cup soccer finals are on TV on Sunday night. The crew will want to be in town for that, so they can't leave on Saturday. Then they will probably have a somewhat convivial evening with their friends, meaning that they won't be in any shape to sail a ship on Monday. So Tuesday, as you can see, is a perfectly logical day.

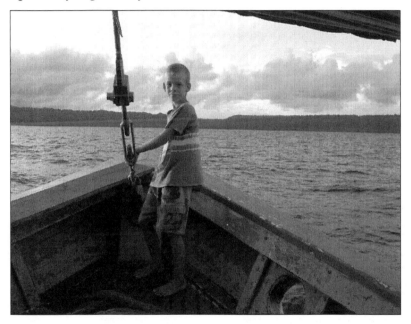

Michael on the deck of the ship headed for Tawatana.

July 3—On the way back to Tawatana

Personally I always think it's a bad sign when you go to the wharf and all the ships are gently bobbing, except for the one you're getting on, which is flopping around like a dying fish. The *Kaona* has a reputation as a roller, and roll she did.

17 hour trip this time. The sea was kinda roughish — the ship going up-up-up the side of each wave and zooming down the other side. Water was splashing in through the windows of the cabin, and up onto the roof of the ship, then dripping down on Andy's bunk. We were well-drugged, so we all slept (off and on anyway) and nobody threw up until about 4 a.m. when the pills wore off. I got up then to visit the rails. When I got outside, the canvas covers had been tied down over the sides of the ship (another bad sign), so that there was only a small gap between two of the covers. The ship was rolling and tossing, and the deck was washing with sea water. As I headed for the gap in the canvas, a towering wave leaped up, higher than my head. I turned my back and got totally drenched. Our friend from Tawatana, Patteson, was sitting on the ship's railing, inside the canvas, smiling and chatting with the crew and apparently having the ride of his life. I couldn't figure out how he was staying on the rail, the way the ship was tossing around. He shouted out to me to just vomit on the deck, because the sea would wash it away. He was right. From then on, Andy sat on a bucket in the middle of the room, passing around the barf pail. When he needed to empty, he just opened the door and dumped the pail out on the deck for immediate flushing action. More memorable moments on the Solomon Sea.

July 29 — Tawatana

I can't believe we've been in the village for nearly a month already. On the other hand, it feels like years. I started to get bored and restless this week, feeling so pathetic and useless. I don't do anything spectacular. I just teach my kids and cook.

I really do think that the best thing I can do right now is support Andy and teach the kids, but it's not always so personally fulfilling as one might hope. And I might as well be an alien from Mars, for all the sense my culture makes to these people. They are so kind to me, so precious to my kids. And yet I want more. I want to know and be known. To share my heart and have someone share theirs in return.

I know in my head that I need to keep realistic expectations. But my heart still wishes for that close friendship. I still want it, no matter how unrealistic it may be to expect it. One of those "not until heaven" things, I guess.

Andy, after long years of experience, can sense this mood in me from a mile off. There's nothing he can do, and we both know it. But Saturday afternoon, we sneak off from the kids and go for a walk along the beach. Even I have been known to cheer up on the beach.

We meet up with this old lady down at the beach, wearing a bright green skirt and nothing else. Breasts hanging down to her waist, tattoos in between her breasts. As soon as she sees me, she cries out with pleasure: "Oh my daughter, oh my daughter." I have never, in ten years, had anyone call me by a kinship term; I hardly know how to respond. Is she really calling me her daughter? But she doesn't just say it once—she keeps repeating it.

She puts both arms around me and hugs me. I've had plenty of women hold my hand out here, but I've never, ever had anybody hug me. She goes on and on, talking and laughing, holding my hand, so happy that I am there. While I of course am doing nothing spectacular—not leading a Bible study, not speaking the language fluently, not even having a cheerful attitude. She is just thrilled that I am there, doing nothing, saying nothing, just there.

This morning I was thinking about her again and I was reminded of Elijah, under his broom tree, telling God to go ahead and let him die. I thought about Elijah, so tired and alone, no longer asking for a blessing, just asking for an end.

Seeing great things happen through him, and too exhausted to ask for anything to happen in him. And the angel came and touched Elijah.

And I thought that this lady was my angel with her hard old hands and her great soft breasts and her tattoos and her pipe of tobacco and her pleasure at my existence. And I realized that, like Elijah's angel, she was the answer to a prayer I hadn't even had the heart to pray.

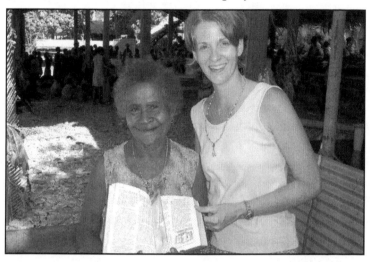

Me with my "angel" at the New Testament Dedication, 2005

August 4—Tawatana

I am

> Tired
>
> Lonely
>
> Desperate
>
> And I know there is no human help for me

I have to

> Keep working
>
> With no one to talk to
>
> For two more years

And I know my strength is gone
I need
    Comfort
    Protection
    Carrying
    And there is no one for the burden.
I am again in that small room
    All walls and no doors
    Waiting for rescue
God give me patience.
Give me strength to wait.

It's Sunday morning and Andy took the kids to church so I could have some time alone. I wrote the poem above, and then I got up to go to the bathroom. Then I went to turn off the CD player, because I couldn't hear the music over the rain on the tin roof. And because the music wasn't helping anyway. I was kind of in a snit about that, honestly. Trying to do the right thing and having it do absolutely no good at all. Just as I put my finger on the player to turn it off, this song started:

Say to those who are fearful hearted,
Do not be afraid
The Lord your God is strong
And with his mighty arms
When you call on his name
He will come and save
Say to those who are broken hearted,
Do not lose your faith
The Lord your God is strong and with his loving arms
When you call on his name
He will come and save

Yes, He will come and save you
He will come and save you
Say to the weary one
Your God will surely come
He will come and save you.
(lyrics: Don Moen)

And now I am sitting on the floor, crying and waiting.

August 24—Tawatana

Miriam died tonight. She was in her 40's and had eight children, the youngest just three or four years old. They say she had uterine cancer. For a year she knew that something was wrong. Finally she went to the hospital in Honiara and they just sent her back home again.

Her sisters sat with her all day today. She kept crying out in pain, asking to be shifted to one side, or to be lifted up higher on the pillows. Her husband went up to the garden; he couldn't stand to listen to her crying.

Late in the afternoon, she said, "I want to go, I want to go, but I'm waiting for Peter to come back from the garden." When Peter came, she died. One of the little girls who was in the room at the time said that she just let out a big breath, and didn't breathe again.

Then everyone in the house began wailing, and the news started to spread like ripples on a pond. Someone ran to stop the boys' soccer game, and to tell the girls to leave their game of *In Water*. Someone else went to beat the drum, just a few loud strokes.

As the news spreads outward, a cloud of silence forms over the village. An unquiet silence, a conscious, swirling force, with a screaming eye of grief at its center. It draws the entire village in. Whole families come, walking silently up the path, past our house, toward the wailing.

We can hear the wailing from our house, mostly low and

droning but with a few high, frantic cries from the closest relatives. "Mother, mother, don't go from me." "Eee, mother, mother, eee, mother."

Outside the house, people are standing or sitting quietly, mostly looking at the ground. Babies are silent, wide-eyed. Children creep around, not speaking, dodging into the house, looking at the body, watching the mourners, learning how to grieve. One young man is lying outside on a bench, moaning, with other young men gathered around him, all crying quietly as they fan their friend.

We leave our shoes at the foot of the stairs and go inside the house. The air is hot, humid—thick with stale sweat and fresh tears. Here, people are weeping openly. Miriam still lies in the small bedroom where she died. The women are gathered around her, and here is the center of the wailing. I can't even see the body, there are so many relatives weeping over her.

Andy stops to talk to Peter, to hold his hand, and to give him the gift of tinned meat and money that we've brought to help with the cost of the funeral week. I squeeze into the back of the room full of women, feeling awkward and useless. Fortunately, no one pays any attention to me. I can just stand here crying quietly in my own inadequate Western way.

Miriam's daughter, Ara, is screaming and crying, lying over her mother's body. Other relatives are holding her, while they wail with her. What she says doesn't make any sense to me. For some reason, she is screaming about cabbage. Later on, we ask someone else about this. Why was she screaming about cabbage? "I don't know either," our friend answered. "Maybe she meant that one thing she would miss was her mother's cooking."

The women want to move the body out of this small room and into the main living area of the house so that the real mourning can begin. But when they start to move the body, Ara screams even louder and faints. Three women carry her outside and bathe her with cool water. "Ara, Ara, think of your baby," they tell her. "Come back and carry your baby."

Eventually we leave the house, and one of our friends walks with us. "I blame Peter," he says. I think that he's talking about the long delay between her first symptoms and when she went to Honiara to the hospital. So I tell him that uterine cancer is just that way. Even with the best treatment, people die from this. Sometimes there's just nothing you can do.

"Why? What causes it?" our friend asks again. Then I realize that he is looking for the true source of the illness. Not the immediate medical cause. If somebody dies here, there has to be a reason. Broken relationships are always the culprit. People don't get sick for no reason. Ill will, anger, curses and sorcery—these are the real causes of illness and death. Peter is known to have been a faithless husband, not much of a support to Miriam. So our friend blames Peter.

August 25—Tawatana

I wake up in the middle of the night with the full moon blazing through my window like an interrogation light. Even the curtains, when I draw them, barely dim the moon. I can't sleep.

Outside there is a strange bird calling, calling, calling. The note is high and rising, an unanswerable question: "Why? Why? Why?" The question sways low, rises. Each "why" ascends a notch up the scale. As the "why" goes higher, it becomes abrupt, demanding, "Why-why-why-why-why-why?"

Far away, another bird calls out. Its cry is falling, soothing, reassuring, comforting. But the why-bird keeps wailing. It moves to another tree, farther away, but I can still hear it asking "Why? Why? Why?"

September 2—Tawatana

A blistering afternoon
Full of sweat and noise and small children
Then
Cave-cool water
Slipping over stones
And I on my back,
My ears underwater,
The world silent and cool.
I open my eyes to
A clean-scrubbed sky
Shifting palm leaves
Sheaves of white orchids
And pure praise
For water
For palms
For orchids
For me, here and now.

September 28—Tawatana

We've been hearing good things about the marriage and family Bible study that we've been doing. Mostly we're hearing that people who are in the study have shared what they've learned with other people. One man went to a funeral in another village two weeks ago, and while he was there he told some of the men about talking with their wives, and especially what we had said about "opening the door" (asking things like, "how did you feel when that happened?") and "closing the door" (giving quick advice, talking over the other person, etc). Some of the ladies in my group went and talked to another lady, who's been separated from her husband for five months. They shared what they had learned, and gave her a paper with the scripture verses in Arosi. A few weeks later, that couple is back together. This past Sunday, a lady from the village of

Ubuna (just about 30 minutes' walk away) happened to be here and sat in on the study. Now she's staying here until next Sunday so that she can go to the study again. Then one really funny story comes from my friend Esther. She really took to the idea of the man and woman being partners, and how God took Eve from Adam's side. She and her husband were having words, and she said to him, "George, I feel like God must have taken me from underneath your feet!" Doing this study with these ladies has been the highlight of this village stay. Just seeing their interest, their eagerness for teaching, and the way they're sharing it with others.

As a result of that study, Andy and I were asked to talk about sex education to the kids at the community high school. We each had about 60 kids. I've known some of them since they were toddlers; it was a bit surreal, and I just stood there and cried before I could even begin my lecture. But I was glad to have the chance to say something that will hopefully be truly helpful to them. One of Libby's friends was in the group and she repeated a lot of what I said to Libby, including the English terms like sperm and uterus. So many young kids are sexually active here, and so incredibly ignorant at the same time. I can just see AIDS taking hold here in the Solomons like it has in Africa.

October 3—Tawatana

The director of our field orientation course told us that the majority of missionaries leave the field because of other missionaries. Another friend said that missionaries are like manure—useful if spread around, but creating quite a stink if heaped up in one spot. I thought these sentiments odd (and certainly inconsistent with missionary biographies)—but then I lived with missionaries for a few years. Now I understand. After another encounter that left me feeling like I'd been hit by a steamroller, I wrote this meditation on Psalm 23:

In the presence of mine enemy
>Yes, she is there
>You don't intervene to remove

Who can look at an enemy when You are here?

Instead you prepare a feast
>When she steals my joy
>You fill me again

YOU prepare
>Food of your choosing
>You serve up forgiveness
>When I would rather gorge myself on grudges

A FEAST
>Lavish, beyond my needs
>I will eat until I'm full and
>Carry the leftovers away for a midnight snack

October 5 — Tawatana

I had a funny cultural moment with a guy yesterday. Billy came up to our house to try to pass a radio message to his wife, who went to stay with her family on another island. He told me what he wanted her to know, which was: come back! I tried off and on for several hours before Andy finally got through at lunch time to give the message. Usually we just have to give the message to the unknown person manning the radio, and hope that they will pass it along. Surprisingly, she herself answered the radio, and when Andy gave her the message, she said sorry but it was going to be "hard". Hard to find transport, and hard to take the kids out of school to come back. So then Billy came back, and I had to tell him that she said it was "hard."

He got really mad and said, "Why did she say that! She should have said something to make me feel good. Even if she wasn't going to come, she should have said that she was coming, to make my feelings settle down. Oh, she's a hard woman. I don't think she has any forgiveness in her heart."

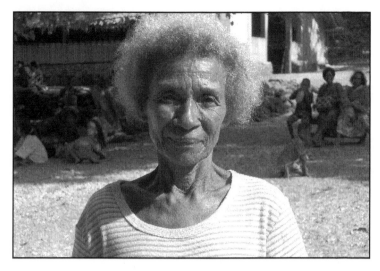

So I said, "You mean, it would be better if she lied to you?"

"YES!" he said.

Billy's mother is very frail and elderly. She fell a few weeks back in her garden, and I think she broke a rib or two. She's been lying in a small garden lean-to ever since, too sore to move back to Billy's house. When we go to visit her, she's lying there in the dark, with her feet close to the fire, the air full of old smoke.

Billy says that a few days ago, she suddenly started talking about death. And she said that she wanted to see Billy's little boy, now gone off with his mother to the other island, before she died. She said that if she didn't get to see this child, her ghost would come back and make the child sick and he would die too. Hence Billy's concern.

Over time we have come to realize that, even as the community as a whole goes to morning and evening prayers at the Anglican church, and even though community members are sincere Christians, ancestral beliefs continue to play an integral part of the way people live and think and behave, on a practical level. When things happen, and I don't understand why, it's often because of what people believe about the spirit world.

One night we were in bed, about to drift off to sleep, when we heard a scratching noise on the roof right over our heads. We realized that one of the kids' kittens had somehow climbed up there, and there was no way we would sleep without getting it back down. Since it was pitch dark, Andy snuck out in his underwear, climbed up a tree and onto the roof, captured the kitten, and came back down. He got back in bed and we were just starting to drift off to sleep again, when we heard lots of shuffling and murmuring right outside our window.

"Andy, Andy," came the call, "Are you okay? There's something big and white up on your roof."

"That was just me," Andy said, explaining to the crowd outside what had happened with the kitten.

As soon as he finished the story, everyone roared with laughter and went back across the yard to sit down again by the cooking fire. For a long time afterward, we could hear them talking and talking, then laughing and laughing and laughing. We thought it was funny too, but they seemed to be getting a disproportionate measure of amusement from the whole thing. The next day, Andy got the rest of the story from a neighbor.

Apparently, there was a group of teenagers out by the fire, when one of the girls, about 15 years old, looked over and saw Andy on the roof in his skivvies. Her first thought was, "Ghost!" She got so scared that she ran away, all the way down to the beach. When the parents heard what was going on, they got concerned, and bravely came over to see if we were okay. Andy and I were fascinated by the idea that a 15-year-old would see something on our roof and think "Ghost" instead of, "What is that idiot white man doing on his roof in the dark?"

And it's not just kids who have that up-close-and-present belief in the influence of the spirit world. One time Andy was visiting with someone when he was offered an ear of corn to eat. When he finished it, he threw the empty cob off into the weeds at the edge of the yard.

"Where did that land?" his host asked anxiously.

"Just over by those rocks," Andy replied.

"Don't worry," came the reply, "we'll get it for you."

When Andy asked why he should be worried, he was told that a snake spirit lived in the pile of rocks, and throwing away food there would allow the spirit to connect with him and make him sick.

Another time, neighbors of ours had an infant son who suffered from all kinds of medical issues. They repeatedly carried him back and forth to the clinic at Ubuna, treating him for malaria and pneumonia and skin ailments. Finally, they were told by the local priest that the ancestral spirit for whom the baby was named was upset. They went through a rebaptism ceremony in church, after which the baby got well and thrived.

Our neighbors believe in the power of the spirit world just about as much as most Westerners don't. All of those beliefs have real-world implications for daily life.

October 6—Tawatana

The marriage and family Bible study ended last night with a potluck supper. Several of the ladies made speeches, some of them with tears, about how much the study has meant to them. Throughout our years in the Solomons, I've been teaching my kids and keeping my house. This year is the first time I've been in the village without a baby in diapers. This is the first time I've been able to do something that I've loved doing, which others have received with such obvious joy. It's been a great gift to me.

October 12—Tawatana

This evening, I sent Jacob across the path with a plate of leftovers, and he was a long time coming back. Finally I heard him coming, speaking *Pijin*, and I could tell that Jean was with him. Jean had brought a big bag of sweet potato down from her garden "for Jacob" and as I stood there, thanking her, she said, "When I think about you all going soon, I just feel really sad. But then I remember that even if we are separated here in this world, someday we'll all be together in heaven."

October 24—Tawatana

The sun is blaring down and the neighborhood kids are sitting in the shade, singing choruses. They sing in three-part harmony, even though the oldest child is only 8 or 9. One kid is singing a high and wild descant, others are droning a bass line. At times the melody is completely drowned by the raging harmonies.

I love their ability to sing harmony, but I still can't get used to their voice quality. It's a strong, nasal blast of sound with all the delicacy of a jet engine when you're subjected to it at close range. "Tuneful shouting" might be the best description.

Still, it's a joyful, joyful noise.

October 25—Tawatana

Early this morning we heard on the two-way radio that the *Kaona* was headed our way—a ship to take us back to Honiara. It might be here as early as Sunday afternoon to pick us up. So we spent the day in serious packing mode.

In the evening we went down to the beach for the farewell party that the village arranged for us. For several days, the men have been out fishing, the women bringing produce down from the gardens; they bought a pig and butchered chickens. They made leis of frangipanis for each of us and seated us at a special table decorated with a cloth and beer bottles filled with flowers. They gave us the best of the food, the biggest portions of fish and pork and chicken, a huge bowl of coconut rice. They made speeches: "We were afraid of you when you first came. We thought all white people were big men—bosses. Then we saw that you just wanted to be like us, so we could come close."

"Your kids are just like our kids. They run around, swim, eat with us, sleep in our houses."

Our next-door neighbor got up and said that he and his wife would really miss our kids. He told how Michael had said to him just that morning, "Hida, I have some little friends, but you are my big friend."

They presented us with a six-foot, quadruple-strand, length of shell money. Each disk is cut by hand from shell, ground into a circle and strung with other disks into finger-length sections. Later the sections are joined into long strands of a fathom each. Each finger-length section has its own name, and the original owner of the shell money can recite the names, recognizing each individual section of disks. Shell money is still used for cash in some places, a dollar per finger-length to pay for your kerosene, salt, or rice at the village store. When a bride is purchased, shell money is part of the price. When customs are broken, shell money must be exchanged in compensation. The strand of shell money that the village gave us is worth 400 Solomon dollars (about $75 US), a small fortune in our area. To receive a gift of such value from people who have so very little is overwhelming.

The party continued with entertainment—singing and panpiping—until after midnight.

October 26—Tawatana

Our neighbors Ben and Elena had us over for a farewell meal. We exchanged stories of our memories together.

Their oldest son, Selwyn, was about 12 when we came to the village. He took our Matthew (3 at the time) under his wing, carrying him around the village on his shoulders, taking him swimming, finding papaya and coconuts. One evening I'd made bean burritos for dinner—always an occasion for us, since rolling tortillas was a production that I didn't undertake too often. I gave one to Selwyn to try. He took one bite, then headed up the path for home. Ben later told us that he'd handed over the burrito and said, "Dad, I think I'm going to throw up!"

Then there was the time that Michael went on a fresh-water shrimp kick. Beniang was the designated shrimp-shooter, taking Michael down to the creek, swimming around underwater overturning rocks and shooting the shrimp with a spear. Then they'd bring the shrimp home and cook them. After several consecutive days of this, Beniang got tired of it, but he couldn't tell Michael "no" straight out. So Beniang would say, "I've got homework."

"But Beniang, it's Saturday."

"Oh. Well, I can't find my shrimp spear."

"Hey, look, it's stuck up there in the ceiling!"

So poor Beniang would give in and go shrimping with Michael.

Now that our boys are a little older, they are repaying the older boys' friendship by befriending Ben and Elena's adopted toddler, Scott. It's a beautiful, full-circle thing to see Scott catch sight of my boys. His little face lights up, his arms fly out, and he comes running to jump into their arms.

October 27—Tawatana

Ben's brother Patteson got his entire extended family together for a meal with us, so that the kids in our immediate neighborhood could say their farewells together.

I can't believe all the cooking and work that has been done for us this week. Every evening it's a huge meal with meat and rice and noodles—things that are expensive, things that local people eat only for special occasions.

We had a lovely, lovely evening, feeling so loved and cared for. Again. Especially the kids. The boys had a special table, the girls had a special table. Some of the kids had even prepared speeches of a sentence or two about special memories with our kids. Then all the kids got up and did an impromptu show for the parents, singing action choruses and quartet-style numbers. We all laughed until we were in tears, at the little ones trying to keep up with the older kids' actions. Our kids sang, danced, and had a night to remember.

I told the other parents, one of my main concerns for my kids is that they've been so happy in the village, I'm afraid that their grief at leaving will be as intense as the happiness they've had.

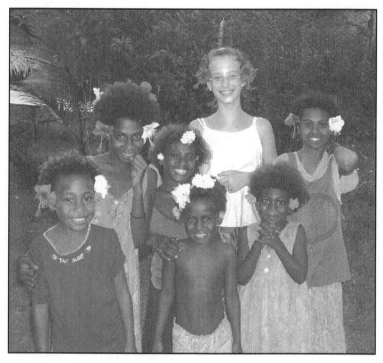

I think the best thing about being a kid in Tawatana is that you're expected to be a kid. Nobody expects you to be mature. They expect you to be childish. If you are grumpy or whiny, nobody takes it as a character defect. They just assume that you are hungry or tired or hot, and they try to help you resolve the problem. You're not expected to be always clean or always quiet. Nobody says, "Stop being so silly" or "What kind of question is that?" They laugh with you, or try to show you what you need to know. They're glad when you eat their food, happy when you want to help in their kitchens, or go to their gardens, or paddle their canoes. Children are not an inconvenience, they're a treasure. And my children have been treasured even more than most. That's something we can never repay.

October 28, Monday — Tawatana

Back to the reality of trying to get transport. Friday, Andy talked to the *Kaona* on the radio and asked them to reserve their cabin for us. They said great, so we renewed the last of our packing efforts. Saturday we tried to get ahold of them all day to check their position, but nothing doing. Sunday after church they answered their radio again, and told us they'd had a change of plans. Instead of coming back to pick us up, the ship had now been pre-empted by 70 high school students heading for home at the end of the term. So here we are, with our house packed up, the solar panels down, and no transport. At least we weren't actually sitting on the beach.

Two other ships are out around the island somewhere, but neither answered their radios. We were all feeling pretty depressed at the prospect of unpacking our things for some unspecified length of time, and then repacking. *Solomons Pijin* has this wonderful word *kansenao* which means something like, "Oh well, there's nothing you can do." It's fitting our situation fairly well.

This morning, we finally got one of the other ships, the *Compass Rose*, on the radio. They said they would be picking up passengers on our end of the island on Tuesday morning. They don't usually pick up passengers down here, so we are only skeptically optimistic.

The *Compass Rose* is larger than the *Kaona*, and rides better in the water, so we would much prefer the *Compass*.

October 29, Tuesday—Tawatana

The *Compass Rose* is still at the far end of the island, doing we know not what. Maybe they will head for Honiara and come past here tomorrow. But meanwhile, the *Kaona* has mechanical problems and is waiting for a spare part to come by plane. Our neighbors tell us that when the high school students finish their term, they start destroying the dorms if they have to wait too long for a ship, a course of action I can fully appreciate at this point. So the great question is—will the *Compass Rose* pick up the students? Will the *Kaona's* part come in time? Will the Bruners ever get off this rock?

November 3, Sunday—Honiara

Yes, we did get off the rock, on the *Compass Rose*, Wednesday evening.

Leaving, we keep the two-way radio on all day, listening for reports of the ship's position. We call the ship a couple of times and remind them that they have 15 passengers waiting here. They keep telling us they will call in for us, so we begin to believe it. When we hear that the ship is at Asimanioha, the next village up the coast, we know that it really is going to reach us today. So clean out the fridge, turn off the gas, wrap the stove in plastic, cut the radio antenna down, shove the lids on the last few boxes. Use the toilet one last time in a bathroom that doesn't roll and slosh. Strap on sandals, grab luggage, head for the beach, sit down and wait. Pretty much the whole village comes to sit with us and wait to say goodbye.

An hour or so later, somebody out in a canoe waves a paddle. He sees the ship coming. A few minutes later, we hear the heavy thrum of the engines and the *Compass Rose* edges around the point, and turns in toward the village. Yes, it's actually going to stop!

But this means that we will actually have to say goodbye. Shake hands, try not to cry too much. Hold my little neighbor Kala one last time. She always runs to me and wants me to hold her. But she is only three. She will forget me and be afraid when she sees me next. I look into faces, remembering all the kindnesses, the acceptance. The times of loneliness were not their fault; I have nothing to forgive; they have given me everything they could. I wonder if I have done enough in return, and I'm pretty sure I haven't. Tears are running down my face, but I don't care.

The ship's dinghy whines away from the ship. The pilot whips the dinghy into the gap between the reef rocks, spins it around backwards, hoists the outboard up out of the water, and rides a wave onto the beach. We chuck in our cargo, with salt water splashing around our calves. The last few handshakes and we chuck in ourselves as well. A gang of guys pushes the dinghy into deeper water, the engine revs up and we're headed out to the ship, watching our friends on shore shrink with distance.

The sea is fine, no problem getting up the side of the ship, ladderless. It's about 8 feet from dinghy to deck, and in rough seas the climb is quite an undertaking. We're glad to have a fine sea, to know that we won't be sick all night long on our last trip out of the village.

Once on board, we find that all the passenger benches under cover of the roof are full. The one cabin on this ship is hot and full of cockroaches as well as human passengers. We maneuver around yellow rice bags, lumpy and soapy-smelling with the dried-coconut product, copra, headed to market in town, and climb the ladder out onto the flat roof. There's hardly anyone out here on the roof, so we set ourselves up behind a clump of empty fuel drums, a windbreak against the night breeze.

The kids immediately set out to explore the ship. The *Compass Rose* has two decks, plus the bridge, so it's a lot bigger than other ships we travel on. They have to go everywhere, see it all. Pretty soon I see the boys up on the bridge, meeting the crew. I can see Matt inside, pointing at instruments. I know the crew is explaining it all to them. A guy from our village is up there too, so I know they won't come to any harm. They will only make friends and probably end up being given food and drinks.

We have two narrow inflatable camping mattresses. We put these down next to each other, and all six of us will sleep side by side, a family of sardines trying to get a little cushioning from the hard deck. We have a couple of old sheets and some grungy jackets to cover up with, nothing special, because the deck of the ship is covered in old dirt and oil, and by morning, we and all our possessions will be as well. We are already wind-blown, splashed with salt water, covered in drying sand.

Friends from the village sit with us. Relatives and friends of theirs come to greet them and exchange betel nut. Libby chats with them in Arosi, and they can't believe a white child speaks their language. One young man keeps laughing and then apologizing, saying, "I'm just so happy when I hear you speaking our language!"

It gets dark and it gets colder and pretty soon we are trying to nest down, kicking each other, pulling the covers off, trying to fit at least two heads on each of our two pillows. Finally we settle down and look up. The sky is full of stars, big and low, so bright they reflect in the sea. Under that amazing sky we sleep and wake, get up when our backs are sore, watch the water for a while, the fish jumping all night, then sleep again until sunrise.

We wake up sore and grumpy and wishing for a good breakfast, since we had crackers for supper last night. But it's crackers again this morning. The kids, since they haven't seen a store in four months, want to spend some of their allowance and they buy warm soft drinks from the ship's canteen. It's 6:30 a.m. I just try not to think about it.

Dirt is ground in under my nails and my face feels like a mud pie. I'm dying for a shower: a hot shower, indoors, with all my clothes off and no one strolling by to chat while I'm bathing.

Mid-morning we arrive in Honiara. Full of noise, taxis, dust, and people. Dry and brown compared to the lush greenness of the village. It's been sixteen weeks since we were last here in Honiara, and sixteen hours since the ship left the village yesterday afternoon. It feels like a lifetime.
The Irony —
When I left my family to come to the Solomons,
I wept.
When I left the Solomons to return to my family,
I wept.

There are pieces of my heart
Everywhere
But somehow, I am whole and well
And thankful.
December 27, Maravagi Resort,
Florida Islands, Solomon Islands
I'm snorkeling in water as clear and blue as a summer sky. The gentle pull of the tide carries me along a wall of

coral. Fish are everywhere—minute clown fish, gray with two frail white stripes; robust parrot fish, teal and purple and lime, scraping the rocks with their beaks; and a wildly colored fish, striped orange and white with a purple tail like God was on acid that creation day.

I drift like a cloud over the world of fish and they ignore me, like I ignore the clouds. Water trickles past my ears, a tiny waterfall sound. My boys are arguing on the beach, far far away. The fish are silent, except for the parrot fish, gnawing on the rocks, a distant scratching, small and insignificant. In the quiet, all my senses are trained on the visual feast: darts of electric blue fish; undulations of white and purple anemones; spiked sea urchins, mounded coral; a blue starfish draped over a rock; a giant clam, patterned in purple and blue, that flinches when I block out the sun; fringed Christmas tree corals, the size of my fingernail, orange and yellow and green and blue and white, clustered on a rock.

God, you're the sky
>Infinite
>Beautiful
>Waiting

I long to fly
>Free in you
>Being what you made me
>Overjoyed

December 28—Honiara

We arrive back from the clean quietness of Maravagi to Honiara, noisy and dusty and strewn with debris. We wait for a taxi on the oil-stained beach, littered with glass and rusted tin cans. A dump of plastic wrappers, broken bottles, pieces of flip-flops marks the high-tide line. But Michael spots a shell hidden in the mess and digs it out—whole and shiny and beautiful.

The Persian poet Rumi puts it like this:
"Where there is ruin, there is hope for a treasure."

Looking back

How do you write about something so horrible, so disgusting that it makes you feel like you've been vomited on? Something that makes you feel like a bag of garbage, thrown on the side of the road?

I didn't know how to do it. I could barely admit it to myself, much less write it down for anyone else to see. So my 2002 journal has a huge missing piece.

My husband was addicted to internet pornography. My husband. Mine. Andy. The missionary. The Bible translator. The one who seemed to never feel the stress, who never seemed bothered by anything. The guy who was great to me and wonderful to our kids. He was looking at pornography and he couldn't quit.

I first found out right after Beth left, in May 2002. Andy's always been an early-to-bed kind of guy, but all of a sudden, he was staying up late, supposedly playing a flight simulator game. I noticed it first the previous January, and I was suspicious, but terrified of saying anything. I just hoped I was wrong. We went back and forth to the village a few times, where there was no internet access, and I thought I had been dreaming it up. But in May, one night I woke up at 3 in the morning and found him again at the computer, and I finally asked, "Are you looking at pornography?"

And he said, "Yes, I am."

I tried to be calm and understanding. I didn't want to make things worse. I'd been unforgiving before, and I didn't want to do it again. I was hurt, but desperately trying to be nice about it.

He seemed to be really sorry. He said he was relieved that I knew, because he had been trying to quit. He said he would quit, now that I knew.

He felt better, but I was devastated. I didn't know how to talk about it, or who I could talk to. My closest friends were gone, and I just couldn't put that stuff in an email. In our mission organization, looking at pornography was grounds for severe discipline, up to and including dismissal from the organization. I had a friend whose husband had had a pornography problem, and they had been dismissed. We didn't want to take that chance, so we didn't tell anybody. Andy tried to be as nice as he could, to make me feel better, and that worked pretty well. After a couple of months, I started to feel less shaky, more myself, and ready to move past it. I thought things had been bad, but they were okay now.

Part 3

The beginning again

Done

Ukarumpa, Papua New Guinea, January 2003

"And go to pieces on the stones/At the bottom of my mind." —Emily Dickinson

"If you are lucky and brave, you will be willing to bear disillusion. You begin to cry and writhe and yell and keep on crying; and then, finally, grief ends up giving you the two best things: softness and illumination." —Anne Lamott

And so it was that in January 2003, we were finished with our village work in the Solomon Islands, and moved to Ukarumpa, Papua New Guinea, to typeset the Arosi New Testament.

We flew the official airline of PNG, Air Niugini, from Honiara, Solomon Islands, to Port Moresby, PNG. In Port Moresby, we boarded a mission-owned small plane for the final leg of our trip to Ukarumpa.

Flying in a small plane from Port Moresby to Ukarumpa was like taking to the skies in the family mini-van. The plane had just enough seats for everybody in our family plus the pilot. We all had to be weighed on big luggage scales, and then the pilot placed us in our seats according to our weight, to balance the aircraft properly. My heavy purse was taken away and stowed in a little compartment out on the wing.

We lifted away from the city, and the coastline quickly fell away as we flew inland over the trackless jungle, looking like a vast swath of broccoli heads, marked only by brown river-squiggles. Then we climbed into the highlands, where waterfalls fell in silvery threads down mountain sides. A rainbow, broad and diffuse, lay on a cloud off to our right as we approached our final destination: a beautiful green mountain valley, home to a large mission center: Ukarumpa.

Arriving in Ukarumpa from the Solomons, we went from the hot, sweaty beach to permanent springtime, 6,000 feet up in the mountains. From homeschooling and DIY medical care to a mission community with a school, doctors and nurses and dentists (oh my), a produce market with year-round strawberries, a Sunday worship service in English, and a store that imported food straight from the Winn-Dixie in North Carolina.

The Ukarumpa mission center was established in the highlands of Papua New Guinea in 1956, and was conceived as a support center for translation teams who would work in the 800-plus language groups throughout the country. Ukarumpa grew from one missionary family in a grass hut down by the river to a small town spreading through the valley and up the hillsides. The population of Ukarumpa was around 1,000 when we arrived there: missionary translators, administrators, school teachers, medical staff, aviation crews; and local employees who worked in the many departments: store, clinic, schools, auto shop, finance office, guest house.

Back in the 50's, mission leaders signed a 99-year lease on this 500-acre property which the government (Australian at the time) considered to be vacant. It was vacant in the sense that there were no houses on it. However, the land had long been used as the fighting ground between two local clans, the Tairora and the Gadsup. This proved to be problematic when the ground was needed for fighting, and there were missionaries living on it, who objected to such behavior. Furthermore, as the property evolved from a grass-covered valley into a small town, the Western-style houses with Western-style belongings inside them made the area an attractive target for local troublemakers, who were known by the deceptively congenial term "raskols" (rascals).

The combination of occasional tribal warfare and frequent home break-ins, plus the risk to women in a country that tops the world's list for rape frequency, eventually necessitated the construction of a barbed wire fence and lookout towers around the perimeter of the property. Papua New Guinean guards, accompanied by trained dogs, patrolled the fence night and day.

We were used to poor security situations and at least at Ukarumpa, there was a person in charge of security and guards who attempted to keep the property safe. To us, the security issues were a small price to pay for the conveniences of a school, a reputable medical clinic, and a store that sold American groceries, stocked on a consistent basis. I had roughed it long enough. I was ready to relax.

After the stresses and difficulties of 2002, my plan was to put the kids into school, let Andy take care of the project, sit down, and breathe. I thought that I survived a really difficult year and that things would now be easier.

My plan, however, was not to be. When we had been at Ukarumpa for less than a month, we got an email from our director in the Solomons, saying he was coming to Ukarumpa for some meetings. I thought nothing of this, until the next email came, saying, "Andy, as soon as I get there, I need to meet with you."

As soon as I read that email, I knew. I knew Andy had not stopped using pornography, and that somehow he'd been caught. I looked at him and said, "You have been lying to me."

And he had. It turned out that what I had known about Andy's pornography use was the tip of the iceberg. I had suspected something was wrong in January of 2002. I was sure enough to confront him in May. But I had no idea he'd been using pornography for six full years, or that he'd kept doing it after we talked about it. I couldn't understand how we had had wonderful times together, like our trip to Brisbane, when he was doing pornography the whole time. The two things just didn't go together in my head.

As I faced up to the fact that he had been hiding things and lying to me for years, I didn't know what was real any more. I didn't know if he really loved me. I didn't know if our marriage would survive. I didn't know if the kids would be okay. I was terrified of what might happen to all of us, and I was in a towering rage with Andy, practically wordless with fury.

"Why would you do this to me, to our kids?"

"It's lust. I can't help it. I've asked God to take it away, and He won't," Andy said in reply.

"That is stupid," I said. "I don't believe you. You better figure this out, and figure it out now."

I had tried to be kind and forgiving when I had initially found out about his pornography habit. I had put my hurt and anger behind the big wall where all my emotions went. But now, the wall was starting to crack. Every time Andy tried to explain how this wasn't as bad as I thought, I would let more and more of my anger fly. I stopped caring if it hurt him. I was angry and I was past caring if he knew it.

Andy had never seen me be so angry, and it scared him to death. Not knowing where else to turn, Andy talked to Marty, a pastor who was visiting for a few weeks from the States. Sitting in Marty's living room one chilly evening, he confessed what he had done in full. He told Marty things that hadn't been discovered, and never would be discovered without his confession. He talked to Marty about his struggle to quit, his pleading with God to take this away, and his decision finally to just give up on God altogether. He talked about feeling like he could never be forgiven for what he had done.

Marty is a man who knows how to wield a 2x4 with love. He agreed that the things Andy had done were sinful, and would have difficult consequences for the whole family. But he was able to show Andy again that God did love him, and that forgiveness was right there waiting. When Andy came home after that meeting, he stopped making excuses for himself, and he was open to other answers about his choices besides "it's just lust and I can't help it." We both felt that he had been healed in a significant way, but neither of us felt that this was a magic wand. It was more like an open door that we could walk through toward more healing.

We had been married over 15 years, but I knew almost nothing about male sexuality in general and pornography in particular. In my very sheltered upbringing, sex was not something we talked about. Rather, it was something we avoided talking about, or even thinking about, until marriage. Even after marriage, we didn't talk about sex. Why would we? I just assumed that if we were having sex on a regular basis, everything was fine in that department.

Since we didn't talk about sex in general, of course we didn't talk about pornography in particular. Even when I confronted Andy initially, we didn't talk about what he was actually doing or why or what his experience was. I didn't want to talk about it. I just wanted it never to happen again.

The only exposure I'd had to any kind of discussion about pornography was Dr. James Dobson's famous interview with a serial killer who attributed his violence against women to his pornography use. That was terrifying and it wasn't helpful at all, in our case. Even though Andy had been looking at pornography for a while, he wasn't a serial killer and he wasn't going to become one. At the same time, it seemed like he was addicted to pornography, since he had tried to quit and couldn't. It was all very confusing.

As I tried to understand what was happening in my world, I began reading a book by Dr. Archibald Hart, called *The Sexual Man: Masculinity Without Guilt*. Dr. Hart had surveyed seminary students, a population much more analogous to Andy than serial killers. He addressed this question: what does normal, healthy sexuality look like for Christian men? He talked about the frequency of sexual thoughts, he normalized masturbation, and pointed out how common it was for Christian men to be exposed to pornography. I would often read a passage out loud and then say to Andy, "What? Is this true?"

While I was encouraged by Andy's repentance, and enlightened by what I was learning about male sexuality in general, I was struggling just to keep going every day. So many difficult things had happened over the course of so many years, and I was barely hanging onto my emotional composure. Andy had seen a lot of my hurt and anger, but I was still trying to keep it in check. I was petrified of what was in the depths of my heart, so I tried not to let myself think about it or feel it. I just tried to hang onto it as best I could. I was so close to the end emotionally that I hardly remember anything about those weeks. I think I must have been like the living dead, just staggering from place to place. I remember spending a lot of time in our bedroom. The room was clad— floor, ceiling, and walls—in dark wood paneling. It strikes me now that it was fairly coffin-like.

I have a daily diary from that time, so I know that Michael played floor hockey and Libby babysat. Matt slept over at his friend Tim's house, and I went to lunch with Jacob at his kindergarten classroom. I have old emails that I wrote to friends at the time, but mostly they just bear witness to my incredible capacity to avoid the truth. It boggles my mind that I could write a long, newsy email to Beth and say absolutely nothing about the reality of what was happening to me.

I do remember going to the community "Hamburger Night," a long-standing Ukarumpa tradition. Since there were no restaurants at Ukarumpa, the high school gym doubled as a fast-food restaurant several Friday nights a semester, where a crew of teenagers cooked up burgers and fries. While the cuisine was hardly notable, and the noise-level in the gym was truly mind-bending, I was willing to go, just so I didn't have to cook.

At one of those burger-and-noise fests, I met my friend Karen. Karen had been through some hard times and healing herself, and I think she could read the desperation on my face. After we met that evening, she started coming over and taking me for walks. I don't remember what we talked about on those walks. I just remember feeling safe with her, always. Sometimes I'd go across the road to her house, where she'd fix me a cup of tea and we'd talk while she worked in the kitchen, making bagels or fixing lunch for her family.

While I was trying to hold myself together, with varying degrees of success day by day, the organization had to decide what to do with us. There were certain prescribed procedures for dealing with a pornography problem, and lots of questions about when and where those procedures should be carried out. The answers to those questions changed frequently, as administrators and counseling staff in the US (our home country), PNG (our current residence), and Solomon Islands (our country of assignment) tried to decide what was best.

While many people were genuinely trying to help, the lines of authority were unclear and decisions were often not communicated clearly. To further complicate the situation, the phone lines went out of order frequently, so we would be waiting for answers to questions, only to find that emails hadn't gone through and conversations had proceeded without our input.

One of the lower-level administrators, who visited with us in person, told us that we had sacrificed a lot for the work and for the goals of the organization, and now it was time for the organization to care for us. We thought that was really nice, and we were encouraged to continue talking to administrators about what our family needed in the midst of this difficult circumstance.

We felt that the best plan would be to stay in PNG through the end of the school year. The kids loved their new school and their new friends. We wanted to let them finish out the school year before going back to the States for the summer and the transition into public school in the fall. Since Libby and Matt were in 7th and 5th grades, and would be entering junior high that fall, I wanted them to have the best shot possible at making a successful transition to public school in the States, sure to be a challenging under the best of circumstances. To me, the best of the probably difficult circumstances meant: finish the school year in PNG, have the summer to transition back to America, enter public school in the fall.

We wanted to finish up the Arosi New Testament project, as well. Andy needed to return to the Solomons for a final check of the Arosi New Testament, and then we were scheduled for typesetting in April in PNG. It seemed to us like a good idea to get the project done, complete the school year, and then go back to the States for counseling.

There was a counselor on the missionary center there in Ukarumpa. A petite dark-haired woman, just a few years older than me, with a big laugh and the ability to be focused and caring at the drop of a hat, Patty was someone I'd met once and liked a lot. I wanted to meet with her, to start processing through what had happened. I thought that would probably get us through the next few months, until we could get back to the States for more in-depth counseling. Since finding out about the depths of Andy's deception, I knew we needed help, and we wanted to get it. We just wanted to do it in a way that allowed us to finish the project well, and to care for our family.

We voiced these ideas, and it seemed like administrators were sympathetic and understood our point of view. At one point, I managed to get through on the phone to a very senior administrator, who kindly stepped out of a meeting in Seattle to speak to me. He seemed to think that our family needs and administrative requirements could both be honored, and I left that conversation feeling respected and cared for.

After a series of conversations via phone and email, one administrator told us that we could make plans to stay through the end of the school year in June. We were very grateful that we had been heard, and Andy began booking airline tickets for June.

A few days later, though, that same administrator emailed to tell us that we would have to leave PNG on April 1. When Andy spoke with this person on the phone, reminding him that he had said we could make plans to stay, he replied, "I said you could make plans, not arrangements."

Suddenly, we had come to a place where nobody would listen to us. We were locked out of the conversation. Decisions were being made about our lives, without our input. We were talking, and then we weren't allowed to talk any more. We couldn't understand how that had happened. I was increasingly confused and frustrated, and I was starting to become very angry.

I was told I couldn't speak to Patty. We were told that when we got back to the States, we would be entering an intense evaluation process, and until the evaluation was finished, we couldn't have counseling. The concern was that we would say something in counseling that was confidential that needed to be included in the evaluation. I said that I didn't really care about confidentiality; I just wanted to talk to the counselor. I would be happy to sign a release so that anything I said could be included in the evaluation. I was told no.

I was trying to figure out what our life would be like next. I was trying to hold it together for the kids, and trying to cope with the fact that my marriage was nothing like I'd thought. I couldn't understand why the organization seemed to be so much more interested in its rules and procedures than in helping me cope with this load that had landed on me.

As much as things had fallen apart, I still held onto the hope that I could somehow bring order and control back to the chaos that was erupting around me. I kept trying to sort it out, fix it, make it better. I thought that if I understood it enough, and made other people understand, then we could get through it with the minimum of fuss. I kept writing emails, talking on the phone, trying to speak and be understood. I just could not conceive of any other way to think, to live, to be.

The more I talked, the less understanding there seemed to be, however. No one seemed to be listening any more. I couldn't understand what was happening. No matter how many times I turned the situation over in my head, it made no sense. Why wouldn't anybody listen and help me?

On Sunday morning, February 23, 2003, we were walking to church, Andy and the kids and I, when I stopped in the middle of the street, shaking, and said, "I just can't do this anymore."

My last little reserve of strength for hanging on and trying hard, slipped away in that moment. It was as if the little canoe that I'd paddled for so long sank without a trace, and I fell into the depths of the sea.

Right then, Karen came out of her house, looked at me, and said, "Are you okay?"

I said, "No."

Major Depressive Episode is the official diagnosis. (I know this term now, as a professional counselor.) What it feels like from the inside is just being *done*. I couldn't think of the future any more, or contemplate the past. Even the bigger world of the present was beyond my comprehension. All I knew was that I was *done*. It was as if the organizational structure of my brain came apart, and all that was left was a terrifying, unquiet darkness.

Andy took the kids on to Sunday School, where they could be cared for, while Karen came up the driveway, put her arm around me, and walked me home. She then called Patty, who came right over. Patty called the clinic, and medication appeared: a little blue pill called Xanax, that magically wiped my mind clean and put me to sleep.

Several months previously, I had written in my journal, "I need to be carried."

And it was true. I wanted to be carried, but I didn't want to fall. If I was going to fall, I wanted a limit to the falling. I still wanted to be able to climb up out of the hole and get things back to normal on my own terms. I didn't like being weak. I didn't like being vulnerable. I didn't want to hurt. Being strong had served me and Andy really well. I didn't know what weakness would be like, but I was sure it would not be good.

I had trained everybody to think that I could and should bear everything. Our whole life in the Solomons was based on this premise: tough it out. Whatever life threw at me—ship travel, life in the village, loneliness, medical emergencies, political coup—I handled it. No matter what happened, I took a licking and kept on ticking.

That day, though, I could not go on any more. I couldn't pretend any more that I was okay. There was no strong, calm, forgiving façade any more. Only a vulnerable, hurting, broken person. When I finally fell, I fell hard.

Once I fell, all the pain of all the years swept over me. There was no ability to reason, to consider, to perceive. I had no sense of purpose, no trust that something positive was coming down the road. Every good thing was behind me, in the past. Somehow I had taken a wrong turn, gotten horribly lost, and could not find my way back. It was every childhood nightmare of being lost, alone, and abandoned. My entire being was consumed by the emotional pain rolling in, wave after wave.

When I slept, I had terrible, repetitive nightmares of being alone and in peril with the children. There were snakes and flash floods and rapists after us, and I couldn't defend us and keep us safe. When I was awake, I had confused and racing thoughts to the point that I couldn't do normal tasks like making dinner. I was so distracted by anxious thoughts and overwhelming sadness that I couldn't read a recipe and follow it all the way through.

Even my tears seemed to come from a different place inside me. These tears were not a cool, controllable trickle. These tears were physically hot: big, fat, bubbling tears like magma welling out of a volcano. Crying these tears left me with no sense of relief. It was as if these tears indicated a deeper, more deadly reservoir of emotion lurking below.

For the two weeks following my breakdown that Sunday morning, Andy sat on the bed with me because I couldn't rest unless he was where I could reach him. While Andy sat beside me, I started to talk to him about the pain. I had lost my capacity for feeling good things, doing things right, being in control, being the good wife, the good mom, managing the home. I was in the dark, and I lost my ability to pretend otherwise. I couldn't protect myself, much less anyone else, from my emotions. The pain and the panic and the inability to process created an undertow that drew me down, time and again, until I thought I would not survive it.

They always say that if you're swimming in the ocean and get caught in a riptide, you shouldn't try to swim against it. You shouldn't try to swim for shore. You should just swim with the current, parallel to the shore, until the riptide eases. After that, you can work your way back to land.

The miracle is that Andy somehow was able to do that with me, in those weeks. He stayed with me in that current of pain. He listened and listened and listened. The more he listened, the more I started to believe that maybe he did love me, and maybe he wasn't going to leave me. As I continued to feel as bad as I felt, he continued to be present with me.

As he stayed with me that way, no matter how bad I felt, I started to feel more at rest. I was still very, very depressed and I knew that, but I was starting to experience some strange moments of peace. Over a cup of tea one morning, Karen shared this scripture with me: *The Holy Spirit prays for us with groanings too deep for words (Romans 8:26)*. And I experienced that to be true. As friends cared for me, as Andy cared for me, I started to experience that God was caring for me, too. I would lie in bed, crying, feeling at the same time that God was with me, loving me.

I emailed a friend about this experience, of being in this horrible depression, with all these terrifying emotions, but feeling that God was with me anyway. I thought it was strange that I could be so angry, so sad, so scared—and still feel that God loved me. "Read through the Psalms again, sweetie," my friend wrote back. "That guy was the man after God's own heart and he wanted to bash people's heads against rocks. We've got room to work here."

A few days later, I was sitting in the living room of our house with another friend, who was also very depressed. I told her about the verse Karen had shared, and I said, "I really do feel that God is giving me things right now that I don't even know to ask for."

As I spoke those words, the phone rang. The person on the other end said, "There's a guy coming to your door in a few minutes. He's wearing a blue shirt and he has something for you." Sure enough, when the knock came, there was the guy in the blue shirt, and in his hand was a plastic grocery sack. In the grocery sack were two small boxes, covered in orange paper and tied with purple curling ribbons, which he presented to me.

"Do I know you?" I asked.

He laughed, and explained that he was visiting from Perth, Australia, where he attended church with Patrick and Sharon Smith, friends from our days in the Solomon Islands. Our last contact with them was breakfast at a McDonald's in Cairns, Australia, just after we had all been evacuated from the Solomons in June, 2000. When the Smiths realized that their friend was coming to Ukarumpa, and that we were there as well, they put together a couple of gifts for us.

To me, it was like getting a present straight from God, at the exact moment when I acknowledged that He was giving me unexpected gifts. And what had God and the Smiths sent me? Chocolate and perfume. I felt, deep inside, that God was showing me something important. He was giving me gifts of pure pleasure, just for enjoyment, just because He loved me.

One morning Andy said to me, "I am not going to the Solomons for the final checking, and I am not going to typeset. I am just going to stay here and take care of you. We'll worry about the project stuff later."

Because of *my* needs, Andy wasn't going to do these things that were so crucial to the project? I couldn't quite wrap my head around it. I liked it, and I felt guilty. How would the Arosi people get their New Testament if I didn't do everything just right? But Andy was adamant. He wasn't going to the Solomons. We would figure the New Testament out later.

In the weeks following my breakdown, Andy began to tell the truth about our situation to the wider world. He wrote a letter to all our colleagues in the Solomons and told them about his pornography use. He wrote to his family. He wrote to our closest friends and supporters. We didn't put details into our general prayer letter; we just said we were going home for counseling. But when friends wrote and asked for more detail, he told his story. *He told the truth.* The more

Andy told the truth about his story, the more I felt free to tell the truth about mine.

In April 2003, we left Papua New Guinea for Dallas, Texas.

Friends came out to the airstrip at Ukarumpa to see us off, including some of the administrative team. The branch director took us aside and said, with great compassion, "Go home and get well. When you're ready, come back. You're welcome here."

Patty stood beside me and said, "This sucks." It truly was a sad, hard day.

I had a picture of God and me, standing at the edge of a dark forest. God was holding my hand and saying, "Honey, I'm sorry, but this is where we have to go."

When we arrived back in Dallas, early on the morning of April 3, 2003, it was our 5th international move in 3 years. We had four kids going into public school with just a few weeks left in the school year. We would have to buy a house, find a church home, and above all configure our marriage into something real and true and good. It seemed like too much to handle.

Things were exponentially better between me and Andy, and I was starting to get some inklings that my interior world could change for the better. Still, I was so sick, so worn out physically and emotionally, that I could barely move. It was like living in the bottom of a pit. I just could not pull myself out. As much as Andy needed to get well and deal with his pornography use, I knew that I needed to walk through my own pain and loss and grief. I just had no idea how to do that. I desperately wanted help.

The counseling war

Dallas, April – September 2003

"We have been socialized to respect fear more than our own needs for language and definition, and while we wait in silence for that final luxury of fearlessness, the weight of that silence will choke us." — Audre Lourde

Within a week of our arrival in Dallas, we began the counseling process that the organization required of us. Because Andy had violated the organization's moral code, we had to be evaluated by the counseling department, before they would offer counseling. As we understood it, the evaluation would determine what kind of treatment we needed.

The very first session in Dallas, I asked my counselor what the evaluation process would be like for us. She said this: "We'll be discovering that together."

Since we had been rushed away from Ukarumpa in the middle of the school year, over our repeated and vociferous objections, this was a shocking statement to me. I thought that if the organization felt the need to remove us from Ukarumpa with such haste, that surely there was a real plan for helping us, once we arrived in the States. Our administrator back in the Solomons seemed to have had a similar idea as well. In an email, he had said that we needed to get to the States as soon as possible so that we could "both get into a supportive counseling situation as quickly as possible."

Instead of a supportive counseling situation, however, we had weekly one-hour meetings, each of us with our own counselor, strictly for the purpose of evaluation. We arrived in Dallas in April, and the evaluation report was written in September. During that time, the counseling department did not offer counseling to us, only evaluation. I had returned from overseas, extremely depressed, yet continued, *waiting for counseling*, week after week, and then month after month, while the organization evaluated. I was left feeling like nobody really cared what happened to me.

Andy was sent to an outside counselor, as there was no male counselor available in the organization's counseling department at the time. After a month or so of weekly meetings, Andy asked his counselor if they could stop evaluating, and move on to the actual counseling. His counselor agreed, and emailed a counseling-department supervisor with the request.

"Don't let them manipulate you," she replied. "The Bruners knew they had to have 9 hours of evaluation, and that the counseling process would take 18 months."

Neither of us had met this person, nor were we aware of her existence as a person of influence in our world, and her information was completely new to us. Our information from administrators, about the evaluation, had said we would need "several sessions" and that we would need to be available for "several weeks." We had tried to ask more about the process when we arrived in Dallas, and were given an answer of stunning vagueness. Strangely enough, even though Andy's counselor didn't seem to understand the required length of the evaluation any better than we did, "the Bruners" were being manipulative.

Unfortunately, Andy's counselor listened to the counseling supervisor. After that, he was wary of everything Andy said, and seemed to look for evidence of wrong-doing everywhere. He criticized Andy for taking our kids to Six Flags, and to our mission organization's swimming pool, where girls would be "scantily clad." He held in suspicion the fact that Andy had been open in sharing his story with people, suspecting some kind of devious intent in Andy's candidness. Whatever Andy said, the counselor challenged as a lie. After a few weeks of such frustrating interaction with his counselor, Andy finally got the original administrator—back in the Solomon Islands—to write and verify to his counselor our version of events. The counselor had to admit that he had misjudged us, and stated that he wanted to build trust again. By this time, though, Andy was disgusted with the whole thing, and the relationship was permanently damaged. Andy just wanted to get through the evaluation and be done with it.

Meanwhile, I was meeting with a woman counselor from within our organization. Before arriving in Dallas, I had expected to go to counseling and feel better. Instead, I would go to the evaluation sessions and feel worse. I wanted to talk about the pornography and the immediate issues that concerned me, but instead I had to answer seemingly random questions like "What was it like, being the oldest of seven children?" I could hardly even think of my extended family, with all the worries about my marriage in my head. I remember replying, "I don't know?"

I started taking two Excedrin before I went in for a session, in anticipation of the migraine that always came afterward. When I told my counselor this, she expressed surprise and stated, "But this is a helpful process!"

"Well," I said, "It's not helping me. It's making me worse."

In fact, it felt like an emotional mugging. I would come home from evaluation sessions, lie down on my bed, and cry. I would repeat to myself, "God loves me, God loves me, God loves me." I knew it was true. I knew God loved me. Beyond that, nothing was clear, and I couldn't understand what was happening or why.

Eventually, I went to my administrator and said, "This is not working for me." He said I needed to talk to my counselor about it.

I went back to my counselor, and reiterated that I didn't like what was happening. She told me, "You don't understand. This is part of the discipline process."

I went back to my administrator and said, "Hey. I'm pretty sure I don't need to be disciplined, since I haven't done anything wrong. Go ahead and discipline Andy, because he did break the rules. But leave me out of it." The administrator agreed that counseling was not a discipline process. He said he would communicate that to the counseling department, and he may have done so, but it didn't impact how the counseling department treated me. I still had to be evaluated, according to their specific rules of evaluation. No matter how badly the process was going — and it seemed to be going badly for everyone — we all had to follow these rules.

Every week, I would walk from our little rented house, down the sidewalk and across the street. Past the building where I'd taken classes as a linguistics student, so starry-eyed and hopeful, down to the single-story brick building that housed the counseling center. As the months went on, just seeing the door of that building made me feel ill.

I continued to be very weak physically, plagued by dizziness and fatigue and anxiety. My nightmares persisted, with a new addition. I often dreamed that the kids and I were alone in a house being attacked by terrorists. Guns were blasting away as I tried to shelter my children in a closet or in a bathroom. I'd be trying to call someone on the phone for help, but help would never arrive. I experienced this same dream, over and over and over. Terrible things were happening, and there was no help for any of it.

Eventually, the relationships were so damaged between Andy and me and our two counselors that a meeting was called for the four of us, plus our administrator and the counseling supervisor. The purpose of the meeting, we were informed, was "so that we can all get on the same page."

When the meeting began, the counseling supervisor asked me to share what my problems were with the process. As soon as I named the first issue, she said, "You just don't understand," and explained to me why I was wrong. At one point in the meeting, I began to cry. I said, "I just want help. Why won't anybody help me?" The four professionals simply sat there and looked at me. I didn't understand it at the time, but I now believe that they interpreted my tears as a further attempt at manipulation.

I was deeply hurt, feeling that no one cared how badly I felt. I was intensely angry, at being treated as if I had violated the organization's moral code, when in fact I was the victim of Andy's choices. I couldn't understand why I couldn't have help, since I was the person most hurting, and I hadn't done anything wrong. The organization's decisions echoed for me all the unjust punishment of my childhood.

I remembered my dad spanking me with a belt when I was in elementary school. As the blows fell, I cried out, "I deserve this, I deserve this." And it seemed to me that the counseling department wanted to hear that same cry from me as they wielded their discipline process. It felt like they wanted me to say that I deserved their discipline. The problem was, I knew for sure I hadn't done anything wrong. In fact, I had been trying as hard as I could, for years and years. Being so mistreated, when I had tried so hard, was devastating to me.

Moreover, I think that I was clinging to the one last shred of my old, familiar life. I had been disillusioned in so many ways. I had lost the dream I had of my marriage; happily ever after had gone up in smoke. I had lost the illusion of who Andy was; the strong, silent, spiritual leader was actually a sex addict. I had lost faith in myself; my strength, my capacity, my whole method for making life work. I was hoping that the mission organization, at least, would live up to my expectations. When it didn't, I was shattered.

It amazes me now, but we stayed in the evaluation process, even after that disastrous meeting. We stayed because our translation project wasn't finished. We had devoted 10 years to that project and we wanted to finish. We believed we had to retain membership with the organization to accomplish that, and that meant going through this required process—no matter how painful it felt. This decision, in fact, was typical of how we thought at the time. Sacrifice, sacrifice, sacrifice.

My capacity to stand up for myself was practically non-existent. I might make some noise, but over and over and over I'd go along with things that I knew were wrong for me. I kept hoping that other people would notice and take care of me, and I was hurt and angry when nobody did that. The months went on and on and on.

The bluebonnets carpeted the earth in April. For Mother's Day, we had a picnic in the park, shaded by cedar trees. Through the long, brutal Texas summer, we watched the grass wither and fade. Then, as the cooling, healing rains came in the fall, I finally, finally understood. I was responsible for myself. I didn't have to lie there and choke. I could get up and speak. I mattered. What I thought counted. I was loved with an everlasting love. I didn't deserve to be treated badly. I had other options.

By the time our mandatory evaluation wrapped up, in September, I was done with our organization's counseling department. Way, way, way done. I wrote a letter to upper-level administrators, saying I would no longer participate in any of their counseling processes. I think I might have said that now I needed counseling for their counseling. I know I said I would seek my own therapy outside the organization.

I figured we would be fired, and I was really fine with that. Andy had come to that place as well. There was just no way we could continue within that system. It had to stop, one way or another, even if it meant that we got fired, and the Arosi New Testament was never finished. I clicked the "send" button and we waited to see what would come back.

After a month, we received a short letter from administrators, apologizing for the difficulty, saying we were allowed to seek counseling wherever we chose, and that they would just appreciate a brief letter from the counselor of our choice, whenever he or she felt we were recovered. We never heard from the counseling department again.

The fact that senior-level administrators finally understood the gravity of the situation, and finally released us from the counseling department, kept us from leaving the organization. That late-breaking show of respect was highly significant at a time when I had felt so disrespected and ill-used. In addition, I had finally figured out that I could stand for myself, in the present, which gave me confidence regarding any future situations that might arise. Once I stopped expecting some nebulous "them" to take care of me, I was okay with taking responsibility for myself in the future. I had learned how to say "no" to others, to say "yes" to myself, and mean it.

Why?

I've spent a lot of time trying to understand why this situation happened like it did. Why would "helping professionals" behave in such a way? Why would God allow me, practically pulverized by life already, to fall into this situation that made me feel so much worse? Why would such an injustice be necessary, when I was already at the end of my rope?

At first, I was just catastrophically angry at all the people who wouldn't listen and who treated me so badly. I didn't understand how they could have done this, when I was telling them it was so bad. I thought they were just crazy and stupid, to have done such a thing. But with time and healing, I've come to some broader understandings.

I think the most immediate problem was my basic misunderstanding of the entire situation. I thought that the counseling department existed to help me when I was broken and used up. I thought I was their client, and that they would be devoted to helping me get better. They said things like "we'll be discovering this together," which further promoted my erroneous belief that my opinion would be central to shaping the process. Instead, looking back, I think that the *mission organization* was actually the counseling department's client, not me.

Our organization, founded in the 1930's, had built its systems around a seemingly endless supply of baby-boomers. In that context, the role of the counseling department had primarily been to make sure that members were healthy enough to serve the organization. If your members were broken, you could always get new ones.

I don't think that the organization set out to treat its members as if they had no value. It's just that there were lots of available members, and the enormous task of Bible translation worldwide took precedence over one little person's pain somewhere in Texas. Therefore, the organization wanted to know: was I too broken to deal with, or did I just need to be replaced? Those were the questions that the "helpful process" was designed to address. As a result, vigilant evaluation of me was more important than good therapy for me.

Lacking this understanding at the time, I expended enormous energy trying to help others understand how the process wasn't helpful *to me*. It never occurred to me to think that "helpful" was more for the organization than it was for me. I thought that being helpful *to me* was the natural, just, and ethical priority, so I spent all my time pushing on a door that would never open.

I don't think the situation was all God's fault. When people behave as though others have no value, that's not God. That's people. Although He could have waved a magic wand at any point in the story, it seems like He rarely does that. From everything I see around me, it seems like He allows us human beings to take our free will and run with it. Often the results are unpleasant, but that hardly ever seems to slow us down.

My own free will was part of the story, too. I exercised my own free will by not standing up for myself, at any number of times in my adult life, which brought me to this place of desperation and despair. Furthermore, I bear the responsibility for not going out and getting my own therapist, right at the beginning of the evaluation process. I knew I needed help, and I should have gone out and gotten it, rather than trying to force the organization to help me. Andy had another large measure of responsibility, for the way his bad choices had impacted me.

It was as if all those bad choices collided into the perfect storm, like the giant tornadoes that devastated Texas each spring. When the storm passed, we were left with rubble and debris spread as far as the eye could see.

When it came time to clean up the mess, Andy was sorry for what he had done, and he was trying to fix it and make amends. That made it reasonably easy for me to forgive him and work on restoring the relationship. Administrators apologized, which helped me feel kindly towards them once again. In later years, I learned that administrators changed the way they dealt with cases of moral failure. They revamped the system and stopped doing the kind of evaluation that had been required of us. That information was validating and healing. I think that administrators genuinely did not understand how bad the situation was for me. They assumed that when the counseling department said that the process was helpful, that it would indeed be helpful to me. It took a long time for them to grasp that it was not helpful to me, but they did understand it in the end. And finally, I had to take part in cleaning up the mess, too. I had to start understanding my own motivations, my own choices. I had to take responsibility to live in the freedom that was God's gift to me.

The Law

Here is the huge irony of my encounter with the counseling department: *they did exactly what I did.* Their stringent system of rules, and the unrelenting application of those rules, regardless of the pain caused, was just an extreme form of the same game I had played my whole life. No matter how innocent I was of any wrong-doing, and no matter how miserable I was in their process, they believed they were doing the right thing, and they could not deviate from those rules. How many times had I done that same thing to myself?

I created rules, I received no grace, I kept going even though I was in agony, all the while thinking I was being helpful and righteous and wonderful. When I encountered the counseling department, the extremity of that particular situation allowed me to finally understand that rule-following was going to be the death of me.

Scripture says that *the sting of death is sin, and power of sin is the law.* *(I Corinthians 15:56)* Sin and death and the law all go together, and I had never experienced that so clearly and profoundly in my life until I encountered the counseling department. The more they applied their law, the more the law emphasized sin instead of grace, the more dead I felt inside, and the more I longed for my freedom.

Without that extreme experience of the law, I wonder: would I ever have gotten free? I tend to doubt it. If I had gotten what I wanted—a nice, caring, sweet counselor to hear me out and love me—I suspect I might have gone back to living by the rules. I might have kept on believing that when I was a good person, good things would happen, and what I really needed to do was be as good as possible.

Instead, I finally learned that my good behavior amounts to absolutely nothing. Even in a situation where I knew for sure that I had done nothing wrong, I had no control. I couldn't fix it. My only hope was to receive grace and trust that God would carry me through. It's very likely, as I think of it now, that the only way to get past my foolish, persistent belief in rule-following was to experience, deeply, painfully, and personally, exactly how horrific rule-following could be.

That experience—that horrible, unjust, law-filled experience—finally, irrevocably broke me from the law. As we ended our relationship with the counseling department that fall, I was starting to get free from the whole dead system of rules and punishment that had governed me every day of my life.

Healing

"Christianity is not primarily a moral code but a grace-laden mystery; it is not essentially a philosophy of love but a love affair; it is not keeping rules with clenched fists but receiving a gift with open hands." — Brennan Manning

"Now, with God's help, I shall become myself." — Soren Kierkegaard

My friend Pam said that life is like a refrigerator, and you just keep putting leftovers away, until one day you realize you don't have any more Tupperware, and also it's hard to get the refrigerator door shut. I was definitely past the point of getting the fridge door shut. Furthermore, there was a bad smell and green stuff was oozing out all over. I was highly motivated to clean that fridge. I knew that the present situation, obviously, needed serious clean-up, but I also knew I had to deal with a lot of things that been left over from years before.

Whenever something difficult had happened while we were overseas—seizures or evacuations or shipping nightmares or farewells—our method for dealing with it was to get through it the best way we could. To me, this meant getting through it with the least amount of emotion as possible. Emotions were messy, and would get in the way of dealing with the crisis. In addition, I believed that any negative emotion revealed a lack of faith in God, a failure to trust. Negative emotions meant I was being less than perfect. The Bible said, *Be ye perfect as your Heavenly Father is perfect.* For many years, I thought that verse was about perfect behavior and being perfectly acceptable to others. Therefore, needing to be perfect, needing to survive, I would stuff down my emotions and get through it. Then, once the crisis was over, it was over. I didn't need to feel bad now that it was over.

I could look back and see that the same emotions had been coming up for me over and over. I would start to explore my thoughts and emotions a bit, and then the next crisis would happen. There was never a time when I was allowed to experience emotions fully, to process all the way through the events that kept crashing down around me. I had to keep making life happen, pushing down those pesky feelings to survive. I could see that this pattern had molded my life.

Feeling the Pain

As I talked to my friends about how depressed and anxious and sad and angry I was, and how much I wanted to get well, people started to give me books. These books became a new community for me, a community of people who knew how to feel, how to grieve, how to be courageous with loss and experience it, rather than locking the emotions away and hoping never to see them again.

In *Traveling Mercies*, Anne Lamott processed through the loss of her best friend to cancer. Lamott, so courageous with her emotions, writes that "the lifelong fear of grief keeps us in a barren, isolated place and that only grieving can heal grief." I knew that fear had locked me in that place. I also knew how painful it had been for me to live in that place, and I could see the destruction that not-being-me had caused to my entire life.

When I locked away all my emotions for the sake of being perfect and having a great missionary project, I became a husk of a person. It wasn't really me. It was just the mask that I thought the project needed. There was no ME present for myself. There was no ME present for my marriage. There was no ME present for anybody. I would try to exist, I would try to speak, but I'd have to shove myself down again to survive in the life I had created. I could see how destructive that was, and I never, ever wanted to live there again. I wanted desperately to be healed. I was willing to grieve, if that's what it took to get reconnected and real again.

In *Abba's Child*, Brennan Manning writes, "Resurrection power enables us to engage in the savage confrontation with untamed emotions, to accept the pain, to receive it, to take it on board, however acute it may be. And in the process we discover that we are not alone, that we can stand fast in the awareness of present risenness and so become fuller, deeper, richer disciples." I definitely wanted to be a fuller, deeper, richer person, and if I had to engage with savage emotions, I was willing to do that. I wanted to really, truly trust that God loved and delighted in me enough to walk with me, even if we walked in places of darkness and pain. Then, believing that God loved and delighted in me, I wanted to be my real self, my whole self, like I had never been before.

So I did what my author friends said. I let myself grieve. I engaged the savage emotions. I didn't do anything to distract myself from the pain. I just cried and raged and stayed in all the emotion. Ironically, as horrible as the situation with the counseling department was, it kept me in touch with a lot of emotion during that time. I couldn't stop feeling angry and sad about how bad the current situation was. The immediate feelings hooked into other feelings, left over from previous experiences that had left me sad and scared and angry. Then I felt those feelings, too.

I did almost nothing productive in those months. I didn't drive the kids to school, because I couldn't remember how to get there. I didn't go to the store, because I couldn't make decisions about what to buy. I hated to meet new people, because they'd ask, "How are you?" and I would start crying. I was so far from "fine" that I couldn't speak the word. When

I was able to attend church, we went to a big church 30 minutes' drive away, where I could be sure nobody would try to talk to me.

Thankfully, Andy and my close friends just kept swimming alongside me in that current of pain. Everybody seemed to be able to accept that this was my work at the time. I had to keep feeling. While it was terribly painful and difficult, I now perceived some purpose in it. There was a path. I was experiencing all these emotions for a reason. I trusted that, as I grieved, healing was going to come. Growth was going to come. And so, as agonizing as it was, for about six months, I just felt horrible. It was not fun. I hated it. It seemed absolutely interminable, and yet I kept knowing, deep in my soul, that these feelings were real and true and necessary. So I stayed in them. Meanwhile, I also knew the shore was still there, and that I would get there eventually. And I had people who stayed with me, so I didn't panic.

After breaking up with the organization's counseling department, I found a counselor of my own. I would go to his office, plant myself on that burgundy and plaid couch, and just say anything. I spilled out all the stories, all the anger, all the pain. My counselor would sit and listen and say, "Wow." There was no judgment, just acceptance that life had been hard and painful and that healing would take time. In that room, it felt okay to tell the truth, to feel the truth, and let it go.

One night, I had the terrorist-house dream again, but it was different. While the house was still under attack, Andy and other friends were in the house with me, helping to defend it. The war raged on, but help had arrived.

Battling the Pornography Habit

While I was experiencing all those long-dormant emotions, we also had to deal with Andy's six-year pornography habit.

Even though he was being very open with me and others, the problem didn't go away overnight. He'd spent years using pornography to stave off stress and pain, and now he had to figure out a whole new way of life, in the midst of the most stressful period of our lives. He'd had that experience of emotional and spiritual healing back in PNG, but he still had to manage the daily temptation and establish a new, healthy set of coping skills. Practical steps like monitoring software for the internet were a big help. Talking to people about it, so it wasn't a big dark secret, was a big help. All those things helped control the worst of the habit. Getting into the depths of the issue, however, was more of a challenge.

Andy told me that he had wanted to quit many times. He had begged God to take away the desire. Finally, he had decided that if God did not care to remove the problem, there was no hope for him to ever do better, and so in his mind he said, "It's just lust. There's nothing I can do." After his conversation with pastor Marty back in PNG, he didn't really believe that any more, but he was still resistant to explanations other than temptation and lust. Digging into those other reasons would require emotional work that he was hesitant to undertake.

I didn't understand or accept the "temptation and lust" explanation; it made no sense to me without an emotional component. If he really loved me and he really was happy in our marriage (which he repeatedly told me), and if it was just lust, I wanted him to quit pornography cold-turkey and never, ever do such a thing again. He refused to promise me that, because he wasn't sure that could be true. He would tell me that he had lust, and I needed to learn to live with that reality. I was not happy with this answer at all.

Andy is naturally a sweet, caring guy, and the porn world with its objectification of women was the farthest thing from the real Andy, but it was as if he'd been trapped in a small room with heavy pot smokers, and he emerged with a contact high. Sadly for him, I wasn't airbrushed, and I wasn't living in the world to wait on his every whim, unlike the online babes. When we began to confront the entitlement he had inhaled in that environment, it was messy and ugly.

One of the big issues that surfaced right away was body image. When I thought about all of the images Andy had seen of other women and their perfect bodies, I felt horrible about myself. I had never been skinny. I wasn't athletic. I started having babies within a couple of years of our marriage, which meant that each and every body part was headed south and I peed my pants if I ran more than six steps. Without thousands of dollars, serious reconstructive surgery, and hourly airbrushing, my body was never going to approach the porno-girls' perfection.

Andy, meanwhile, had deep-seated body-image issues of his own. He had been skinny all his life, and teased unmercifully about that. Even after we were married, people would say things to him like, "Wow, do you have to run around in the shower to get wet?" Of course, it was hugely impolite to make remarks to someone who was overweight, but if you were underweight, it was open season. In addition, he went through puberty late, and was mistaken for his mother on the telephone until he was a junior in high school, an almost-daily humiliation.

One of the ways he dealt with his own insecurities was to project anxiety onto me. He would observe that my stomach seemed to be a little rounder, right after Thanksgiving. Or he would observe that I hadn't gone to the gym in a couple of days. He felt perfectly entitled to say these things to me, as if I needed this information.

For a while, I listened and felt bad and tried to be skinnier and more toned. But I could only do so much, and it never seemed to really make him happy anyway. After a while, I started to see a pattern between his dipping back into porn, and then telling me I needed to change. Once I realized that connection, I knew it was boundary time. I told him that every time he commented on my weight or body shape, I would assume that he had been looking at pornography again, because that's when the entitlement would be most prevalent. I told him that when he said I need to go to the gym, I would tell him that he needed to go to therapy. It was bad enough for me, living in a world where a size 8 qualified a girl to be a plus-size model. I didn't need my own husband making it that much worse. I would eat normally and do a normal amount of exercise, but after that, how my body looked was not his problem. His problems were his problems, and he had to work on his problems. I couldn't work on his problems for him.

I remember one night we were having one of our worst fights ever, after he'd confessed to looking at porn again. He was saying "It's just lust" and I was saying, "You've got to be kidding me," each of us deeply entrenched in our own position. As the argument escalated, I realized I had to stop myself. I said to Andy, "Okay, I'm just going to listen now. I just want to understand what you're trying to say."

I didn't agree with what he had to say, but I wanted to understand, and I wanted to get us working on the same team. I became deeply convinced that we had to turn the conversation away from our disagreements about behavior and motivation. We had to establish some deeper understandings, which I hoped would then impact what happened on the surface.

That didn't mean he could just throw himself into the depths of pornography addiction and I would be fine with it. He had to work on the addiction. He had to work hard. I wasn't going to be silent, either. I was going to state my boundaries and hold to them. However, if he was genuinely taking responsibility for himself, then I had to accept that he was working on his issues in the way that he felt was best. That wasn't going to result in perfection, today, but he really was working on it.

I think I was able to accept that compromise more readily, because he was accepting me while I was working on my mess of depression and anxiety, in my own way. Eventually, we agreed to this. He had to own his issues and work on them himself, while turning toward the relationship emotionally. I had to own my own issues and work on them, while turning toward the relationship emotionally. As long as we were each turning toward the relationship, we had to accept the other person in good faith, wherever they were in that moment.

Welcoming Our Own True Selves

As we turned toward the relationship, we each had to accept and welcome things about ourselves, and about the other person, that we hadn't before. A huge part of that was accepting our personality traits. We are almost totally opposite in our temperaments. Andy thinks first, and he thinks in a linear progression to a logical conclusion. He may, at some point, experience emotions about a situation. I, on the other hand, have emotions, first, foremost, and unfailingly. Logical conclusions may result at some point. Or not.

I had spent most of my life trying to figure out to be *good enough*. Now I had to learn how to be *me*. I had to learn that my way of being was acceptable. In fact, my way of being was beyond acceptable. God had made me this way on purpose. My way of being was not a defect, a weakness, or something we just had to learn to work around. It was, instead, a strength, and a resource that our marriage desperately needed.

Our marriage had had a lot of life on the surface, a lot of motion and production, but it badly needed a richer emotional life. Without that, in the long run, it satisfied neither of us. I had thought that Andy's way was the best way, so I had tried to be Andy. I denigrated and devalued myself as a result. And that, I came to see, was a constant slap in the face of God, as if He had made me wrong and I had to fix myself.

I had to learn to accept and welcome my own true self, the self that feels first and always. I had to learn that, for me, feeling IS thinking. When I accept my feelings, I find that they are telling me some kind of truth. When I start with my feelings, I can follow them down deep into my soul, where Love lives and moves and has its being inside me. My feelings are valuable, because they are attached to that deep understanding.

We also had to accept that Andy is valuable just as he is. In many ways, his natural passions were denigrated just as much as mine were. For every "should" that I experienced, he experienced one too. There were a lot of religious cultural standards he was supposed to live up to, that just didn't fit. "Being spiritual" in a standard religious sense is just not something that fits his personality. As the "spiritual leader" and the "head of our house," he was often asked to speak in churches or to lead a Sunday School class. He hated it. He did it sometimes, when he absolutely had to, but it was always difficult and unpleasant for him. However, there was an ongoing expectation that he would want to do this, or be gifted at it, if he was a real "missionary man."

While we were throwing my "shoulds" away, we threw his out, too. He was allowed to feel how he felt, to the measure that he felt it. He was allowed to be quiet when he didn't want to talk. He was allowed to feel happy as the kind of husband and father that best fit his own individual personality. We both became passionately committed to embracing him as he is, and not holding him up to arbitrary cultural standards.

That included not forcing him to do therapy my way. My way was to bring all the emotion, all the pain to the front, experience it, and be healed. Andy's way to healing was the practical way. Be honest. Have internet filters. Take care of absolutely everything in the house, so I could do my emotional work, and not have to worry about practicalities. Listen to me and love me, no matter what wild emotion I felt at the time. Paint the living room, over and over, until I found the right shade of blue.

I didn't have to be Andy. Andy didn't have to be me. We each got to be ourselves.

Bearing the Pain

During those months, we talked together every single day, sometimes for 20 minutes, sometimes for hours. We did not watch television at all. Our kids were still young enough to have a bedtime, so when 9:00 hit, the kids were in bed and we were talking. Andy began our tradition of a nightly bubble bath, where we sat together, every single day. That's how we spent our evenings, for months and then years. Talking to each other. Making up for years of lost time. Accepting the reality of each other in a way we never had before. Sometimes we fought. Often we wept together.

In the whole, long process, I had to hear a lot of stuff I didn't want to hear. Andy had to feel a lot of things he didn't want to feel. Slowly, though, we found that all the painful conversations were making changes in both of us. I wasn't so afraid to hear hard things. He wasn't so afraid to feel hard things. We developed an ability to bear pain *together*. Neither of us thought we were going to find a place of sinless perfection any longer, but we were finding ourselves in a place of bearing it together.

As we talked those many hours, Andy realized that being the youngest of five boys had seriously impacted his self-worth. He always felt young and foolish, ignored and overlooked. The stress of the translation project and the distance that developed in our marriage evoked similar emotions. Pornography provided an enticing place to escape all that pain. Once he started looking at pornography, he was ashamed of what he had done, which made him feel worse about himself. When he felt worse about himself, he wanted to feel better, and pornography filled that need. With the cone of silence around sexuality in our conservative Christian world, he felt that there was no way he could talk to anyone about his struggle without causing wide-spread panic. The silence and hiding and pretending added another layer of stress, which in turn caused more need for the pornography use.

As our marriage began to heal and grow, we each drew strength from it in order to face our individual issues. As we healed individually, that gave us strength to continue working on our marriage and our family. Instead of the old vicious cycle that brought disconnection, we ended up with a growth cycle that healed a lot of hurt in both of us, and gave us the courage to keep on healing.

Responding to Stress

We started thinking aloud together about how we had each responded to the stresses of life overseas. I needed to talk things through out loud, while Andy needed to think things through inside. The more stressed I was, the more I needed to talk. The more stressed he was, the more he needed to be alone with his thoughts. Lack of understanding in that one area of difference had created a world of hurt and emotional separation for us.

We each revealed the feelings of incompetence we'd hidden from each other. I felt incompetent in the translation project, so I put all my efforts into caring for the family and our home, where I could reasonably expect some success. Andy felt incompetent to deal with emotions, and verbalizing his thoughts. The more difficult his thoughts and emotions became, the more he avoided me and put all his efforts into being successful at work.

Evaluating the Call

Both Andy and I had been steeped in Scripture our whole lives, with family devotions and Sunday School and Bible classes in college, to say nothing of our years in a Bible translation project. We had a lot of good information in our heads about What God Said. Much of our healing process was learning to go beyond head knowledge of scriptural principles, into a solid life of tangible health and wholeness. We knew that the way we had lived our life, even though it was framed as "God's will" and "serving God," was far from healthy.

We said that God loved us, but we made decisions that devalued members of our family. If God loved us, we should behave accordingly. We should live a life of love that valued all of us.

We processed through decisions we had made, like going to the village when Michael was four weeks old.

"That's the stupidest thing we ever did," I said.

"Why?" asked Andy. "Nothing bad happened."

It took a bit of explaining, but finally he could see that bad things had indeed happened. Bad things had happened *on the inside of me*. I ended up feeling anxious all the time, and ignoring it all the time. The constant buzz of anxiety thrashed my brain chemistry almost to death and set me up for major depression when stress kept happening.

We came to agree that "nothing bad happened" was perhaps not the best standard for evaluating our decision-making processes. Instead of making decisions that didn't actually kill anybody right this minute, we wanted to make decisions that would promote long-term health and sanity for our entire family, including me.

We started to question what "God's call" really meant to us. We thought we were listening to God. In reality, though, a lot of times we were listening to whatever would feed our egos and make us feel better about ourselves. Andy's love of adventure often failed to account for my needs for stability and connection. As long as new things were happening, he could be happily absorbed in those challenges, too busy to face the emotional work that needed to be done in the family. I was terrified of punishment and imperfection, so I was always trying to be super-good so that nothing bad would happen. I was trying to be the perfect wife and missionary, so I ended up going along on Andy's constant adrenaline quest, even when I knew those exploits were not best for me or the kids.

Being Whole and Together

We had both grown up in a patriarchal system that said, "Men speak. Women are silent." From that system, I grew a whole inner world of personal unacceptability. My inability to experience my emotions and my inability to speak truthfully, were part of my "women are silent" mindset. As Andy and I talked together, as my voice became a welcomed and invited part of our relationship, and as our relationship became a place of nurturing for us both, we realized how much we had missed, by living within that very rigid male-female separate-role system. We felt, more and more, that what we really wanted was to be whole and together. Our unity became the most important thing to us.

The more we experienced the value of each other, the more confident we became in ourselves as a couple. We brought completely different perspectives to any situation that we faced. When we made a decision, together, we knew we had considered probably all of the existing possibilities, just because we each saw things so differently. The more we respected and treasured those differences, the stronger we grew, and the better our decisions became. We could still retain a fair amount of forward motion, thanks to Andy and the way that he propels our lives into productive paths. But my fully-present self could contribute an emotional depth and meaning to our relationship that hadn't previously existed.

It became almost impossible for either Andy or me to imagine making a decision that the other didn't support whole-heartedly. We each had a sense that we truly needed the other person's perspective. I knew I need Andy's linear, logical thought patterns. He knew he needed to hear how I felt. His thoughts and my emotions came together, into a powerful whole that nurtured and valued each of us separately, and both of us together. Whenever we came to a decision point and we didn't agree, we knew that we just needed to keep talking it through and loving each other until we came to a conclusion that supported our unity.

The Good Christian Woman gets some Boundaries

As we worked on our own interior worlds, and the inner world of our relationship, that impacted the outside world. One of the most immediate changes came in the world of boundaries, which I had long recognized as an area of challenge for myself.

My lack of boundaries, on the surface, perhaps made me seem like a spiritual servant, always caring for others, but in fact it was a lie. My lack of boundaries was based on what I thought would make me more perfect and acceptable to others, rather than what was real and true and honest. I thought back to the time in Tawatana when Billy told me that his wife should lie in order to preserve the relationship. I could see the lie in his culture, and I could judge it as bad, because the Bible says "thou shalt not lie." But I often found myself doing the exact same thing for the exact same reason. I wasn't telling the truth. I wasn't being honest. I was lying, most of the time, about how I felt and why I did what I did, so that other people would think I was a good person and approve of me. There was very little truth in me.

Just like I thought Andy's surface behaviors were attached to underlying emotional issues, I figured mine were, too. I could stop the behavior, but, in keeping with my emotional perspective on life, I wanted to understand where my behavior came from, so I could work to heal whatever pain was driving my behavior. I didn't want to spend my life picking the leaves off the tree. I wanted to get down into the roots and dig the whole thing out and be done with it.

About a year after our return to the States, I went to a family funeral. As I listened to the stories being told by older family members, I realized that my extended family had been severely traumatized by addiction and abuse, three generations past. Here I was, an adult with children of my own, and I didn't know this intimate history of my own family. Families of alcoholics, though, are fabulous secret-keepers, and it was only as the last of a generation passed away that a few truths could be quietly acknowledged.

As I pieced together the various recollections I heard with the patterns I had observed in my family over time, I realized that my family's answer to all the chaos was to turn to religion and its rules for control. People got saved, because anybody who had been thrown down the stairs knew for sure that they needed to be saved. Then people forgave and forgot the best way they could. They even moved across country or halfway around the world in order to forgive and forget. They served and ministered and did a bunch of good, in order to forgive and forget. But they didn't know what to do with all the pain that lingered, after all the forgiving and forgetting and moving and ministering. Without the direct experience of grief, even generations later, the emotions were still there, the fear and the anger and the pain. Along with all that emotion, there was a terrible and tangible fear of messing up. Truly horrific things happened when people messed up. Nobody could mess up, ever again. Out of the pain and fear grew an insatiable need for control.

That's where the family history of addiction and abuse impacted me. I wasn't an addict, but I started to think that codependency might be a bit of an issue for me, especially once I realized that the list of codependent characteristics described me perfectly. Feeling responsible for everything. Feeling angry, victimized, and used. Anxious. Overachieving. Feeling not good enough. Fearing rejection. Blaming, denying, controlling, withdrawn, hopeless, depressed. Yup. That was me, alright.

In an addict's family, nobody wants the addict to feel bad, because when he feels bad, he will use and abuse. There is enormous effort, on the part of the rest of the family, therefore, to bear the weight of the addict's happiness and emotional stability. Even though my parents and even grandparents weren't addicted, they had grown up with those patterns, and they passed them down to me. In fact, there was a family phrase for that kind of codependent pattern of behavior: "She was a Good Christian Woman." The Good Christian Woman kept others happy at all costs. God forbid someone else should be unhappy. Chaos could ensue.

My personality played into the whole sad scenario. I was naturally attuned to my own emotions and the emotions of others, which made me highly susceptible to codependency. In a family where Good Christian Women spend their lives keeping others from feeling bad, I was a born expert at sensing the emotions of others, and I quickly learned to pacify those emotions with great expertise. Since I was also a perfectionist, and so good at being codependent, I loved being able to make others feel better. It made me feel competent. It distracted me from my own problems, when other people were so crazy and needed me so much. Being codependent had a million rewards, until it almost killed me in the end.

Having stood on the edge of the abyss, I knew I had to change. I had, for years, ignored the sick feeling in the pit of my stomach when somebody said or did something that was just not okay with me. I'd try to pacify, but after any number of emotional black eyes, it didn't feel so good any more. People would tromp over my boundaries a million times until I finally got up the courage to say, "No?" I would say no with my question mark, and they'd shout me down, and we'd be back where we started, me with my bruised and beaten emotions, all over again. Only I got more and more angry, which turned into deeper and deeper depression.

I read the *Boundaries* book again, and this time, with the force of desperation, things stuck with me. I knew that Jesus often withdrew from the demands of the crowds, and I started to realize that I had to follow that example or I would literally die.

My new mantra was, "Do the right thing and learn to live with a little guilt." In the past, I would feel guilty if I didn't do what I knew other people wanted me to do. I thought that the guilt was the truth, so I would listen to it. But I was learning that my guilt-o-meter was fatally flawed, absolutely unhinged, and totally untrustworthy. I knew I couldn't listen to the guilt for one more minute and survive. Guilt was a lie. I had to learn to listen to Love instead.

I started being more consciously aware of what I wanted and didn't want. Then, I started to say what I wanted and didn't want. No more, "No big deal." "No big deal" too often meant that I was lying and devaluing myself and trying to pacify others again.

A new Starbuck's opened around the corner and I went in for my favorite thing, a chai tea latte. The brand-new barista put a shot of espresso in my tea. I didn't want a shot of espresso in my tea. I took it back. She told me that chai tea was made with espresso. I said I didn't want espresso in my chai tea. She said that was the way it was made. I said, "Well, I need mine made differently." She finally saw it my way. This was a huge victory for me, as in the past I would have just taken my chai with espresso and been unhappy. Instead, I was able to keep politely expressing my preferences until I was heard.

Once I had practiced on people like the Starbucks barista, I started getting bolder with people closer to home.

I had an acquaintance who wanted her boys to be friends with my boys. The family was struggling and the kids weren't doing well. Perfect for me, of course. I wanted to help them. We met for a few play dates, but my boys didn't like playing with her boys. Michael said to me, "Mom, they don't want to play with me. They just want to break my stuff."

"Awesome," I thought. "My seven-year-old has better boundaries than I do." The next time she called and asked if they could come over, I had to say, "I'm sorry. This just doesn't work for us." Then a couple of days later, she came and rang the doorbell, and with her two boys standing there, said they wanted to play. I felt so sorry for her kids. But I knew what my kids' boundaries were, also. Her kids stayed that day, but I had to tell her that they could not come again.

Many times, as I started being aware and speaking about my wants, I wondered if I was being selfish. I felt guilty a lot, but now I knew the guilt was a lie, and I needed outside consultation, to check that my boundaries were okay. If I couldn't tell if I was being healthy or selfish, I would talk to Andy about it before making a decision. He would inevitably tell me to say no when I wanted to say no. I might still feel guilty, but more importantly, I felt empowered and cared for like never before. I had learned so long ago that God delights in me. As I learned when to say "yes" and when to say "no," I was living out God's delight and my freedom in the real world. No more rules. No more pressure. Just love. It felt like flying.

Perfectly Normal

As I kept practicing, the world kept turning. My junk was about as much as I could deal with, most days. Other people would just have to deal with their own junk, like I was having to deal with mine. If I made mistakes, that was part of being human. Only God was God. Only God was perfect.

By accident, one day, I happened to read through the passage that had given me so much grief, the one that says, *Be perfect, as your Heavenly Father is perfect. (Matthew 5:48)* I finally read the context. The passage is talking about how much God loves us, and everyone else. The verse tells us to be perfect in that way: in our love for each other.

I was starting to feel, for the first time in my life, that I might have genuine love to give away. It seemed that in the past I had been a counterfeiter. I didn't really believe or experience that God loved me, but I was supposed to love other people anyway. I gave and gave and gave, thinking it was love, but often I was giving out of emptiness, a fake love. But now, the more I received love from God and from others, the more I was filled full of love, and the more I could choose to genuinely give to others. Because I could really say no, then I could really say yes. Furthermore, I could trust that God was the source and supply for others, not me. When I said no to someone's request, I trusted that God would meet that person's needs, even though I could not. God's love was perfect for me, and perfect for others as well.

Somebody asked me, "When will you be back to normal?" And by that time, I knew. I knew it would be NEVER. I would never be back to normal, because my old normal was bad for me, it was bad for our marriage, and it was bad for our family. Andy didn't want to be the old normal, shut-down, lonely person he had been, either. Neither of us wanted to go back there again, but that was hard for some people to hear and understand. Our life had looked fine on the outside to them. They had no idea how deathly ill it had been on the inside. Letting others be uncomfortable with the new us was just another way to practice good boundaries. In the past, we would have changed or at least hidden what made others uncomfortable. Now we could just let them feel how they felt. We knew, together, that we were getting healthy. We loved our new life. There was no going back.

The Kids

Our return to Dallas meant that our kids were dealing with their third school situation—and third country—in one school year. They had been home schooled in the Solomon Islands, attended a small mission school in Papua New

Guinea, and then went into huge public schools in suburban Dallas county in April.

They were at four different ages and four different stages of life and the multiple moves and family upheaval impacted each of them differently. To say that it was an emotional disaster zone is not an exaggeration. Of course they each had their own losses and griefs to bear, and then life kept happening to them as well.

Matthew was bullied at school on a regular basis, and none of my calls to the school seemed to impact the situation. They weren't willing to do anything about it, not even the day that he came home with a bleeding bald patch on his head, where a kid had yanked out a quarter-sized hunk of hair. There was not much we could do about it, except cry through it, and wait for the healing.

One of the enormous blessings of being in Dallas—in fact the whole reason we had chosen to come to Dallas—was that friends from our Solomon Islands days had settled there as well. When school had been particularly bad, I could call up my dear friend Roxanne and say, "My boys really need friends right now. Can we borrow David and Mark for the afternoon?" David and Mark would come over and hang out and make our world a better place.

Andy had taken over as Mr. Mom at that point, doing everything for the kids for many months. If they needed school clothes, he went and got them. If dinner was going to happen, he made it. He picked up kids, he dropped off kids. He kept everything going while I was too sick to remember how to get to the store, much less make a decision once I got there.

And then he did something truly heroic. He told our kids the truth about his struggle with pornography. He told the older two at the time, and then waited to tell the younger two when they got a bit older.

When he told me that he wanted to tell the kids, I was really opposed. I thought it would just hurt them more, at a time when it seemed to me that they'd had way more than enough. However, he felt strongly that he should tell them, and he was right. Genius, in fact. Not that it wasn't difficult. Or painful. It was. Terribly. But it was absolutely the best thing he could have done. It was honest. It was about real relationship. It was about vulnerability and connection. It was totally in keeping with our growth and healing.

Telling the kids meant that we were not hiding things from them. They knew what was going on. They didn't have to make up stuff to explain the emotions in the house. Our kids were free to be angry with us, but they didn't have to blame themselves.

Telling the kids meant that they weren't responsible to fix the family. This was an adult problem, the adults were taking responsibility, and the adults were doing what needed to be done to fix it. The kids could be mad at us, but they didn't have to fix the family.

Telling the kids meant that we admitted that we were human and imperfect. It would be nice if we were perfect, and they never had to deal with reality. But the perfect ship had sailed. So we told the truth and we dealt with it.

Andy found us a house to buy, right next to a park with a lake. It was the perfect setting for our family, since the kids were used to having lots of space to explore, and their new suburban setting was a lot more restrictive than they liked. We got a set of walkie-talkies so that the kids could roam the park and stay in touch with me, too. One day Michael had been out in the park for a while, when he called on the walkie-talkie.

"Is it okay for me to get in the water?" he asked.

"No, no, that water is really dirty. Please don't get in it." I said.

"But Mom, there's a baby turtle," he pleaded.

I ran over to the lake and found him lying on the dock, where he'd been for about half an hour, patiently waiting for this baby turtle to drift close enough to catch. It was within inches by that point, so I held onto his legs while he stretched a bit farther and managed to capture it. He kept it for several weeks, and then released it, feeling it might be lonely by then.

The turtle put the kids in mind of other, more interactive pets, so we got a dog, a little poodle mix from the animal shelter, who was always ecstatic to see the kids when they came home from school.

Slowly, we all started living again, instead of just surviving from one disaster to the next.

Fear and Hope

"Here is the world. Beautiful and terrible things will happen. Don't be afraid." — *Frederick Buechner*

We visited Tyler Street United Methodist Church as a family, early on in the church-hunting process. Friends went there, and we'd heard it was great. When we first visited, I was so broken that I couldn't handle people talking to me and expecting coherent conversation. We went instead to a big church with great music, a fabulous sermon, and nobody who wanted to talk to us. It worked until the kids got invited to a youth event at Tyler Street. They loved it, and were adamant that this was the church they wanted to attend.

While the two older kids had youth events and budding friendships, the two younger kids were not as ready to venture out into any place where the parents were not. They wouldn't go to children's church, and they sat in the pew with us and rustled around as little kids do in pews.

I felt badly about this, because when a church provides children's church, it's generally because they want your children to go there and not rustle around in the pews. But our kids were in school all week, and that was pretty much what they could handle. On Sundays, they stayed with us.

One Sunday during the sermon, one of the boys was playing with a couple of quarters. One of those quarters dropped out of his hand and rolled, down the 100-year-old sloped wooden floor, to the carpet near the altar rail. I was mortified. After church, an older gentleman approached me and I thought, "Well, he's going to tell me about children's church or the cry room or some other place for us to be, instead of rustling around in the pews."

Instead, this man said to me, "We just love having your family in church with us."

People loved us when we weren't perfect, and that's how we became Methodists.

I love stained glass and organ music and the Apostles' Creed and The Lord's Prayer. I love kneeling at the altar rail for communion. I love the church calendar and observing traditions passed down through the centuries. I even love Lent.

My love affair with Lent began on Ash Wednesday, 2004. I didn't know what Ash Wednesday was (it's the first day of Lent), and I wouldn't have gone, but the choir was singing. Since I had just joined the choir, there I was.

One of the things we did, that Ash Wednesday, was to write on an index card what we were giving up for Lent. Then we would nail the card to a huge wooden cross at the altar rail.

I personally felt like I had already given up plenty of things in my years in the Solomons, and I was just beginning to enjoy Coke and hamburgers and TV again, so I wasn't interested in giving any of that stuff up. I sat there with my card, thinking, "I have to nail this thing to the Cross, so what am I supposed to give up?"

And this is what I heard: "Fear."

That was a hard one. So many difficult and painful things had happened, and I was used to living in a state of anxiety and watchfulness. But I heard that I should give up fear. That's what I wrote, and that's what I nailed.

A few weeks later, I was at a women's retreat which happened to fall on the weekend of Palm Sunday. The first question they asked at that retreat was, "What does God want to give you?"

And this is what I heard: "Hope".

That was also a hard word for me to receive. All my hope in the past had been based on my own behavior, my own goodness. I said I hoped in God, but mostly I hoped that I would be good enough to keep the bad away. My experiences over time had forcefully demonstrated that my good behavior was no defense against the badness lurking in the world. I knew in my head that I could not hope in my own goodness any more, but letting go of that in my heart was not easy. That day, all day, I wrestled with shedding the control that felt so safe and secure: my performance, my perfection, my goodness, my enough-ness.

Later that evening, we shared communion, with candlelight, bread, juice, silence, and love in the room. Pastors from the church were sitting off in the corners, ready to listen to anyone who needed to talk.

I went and sat down in front of a pastor I'd never met before, and haven't seen since. I wanted to tell him a little of my story, but all I could say was, "I'm a missionary," before I started sobbing.

I sat and cried for a long time, and the only other thing I could get out was: "When will it ever be enough?"

That man looked at me and said, "It is enough already."

With those words, a sense of freedom and peace came over me, like I had never known. For the first time, I actually experienced the reality of Jesus' words, "It is finished" on the cross. Those words covered everything. Everything is done already. God has taken care of it. Sure, there is work, and I can participate. But I'm going to walk in the cool of the evening and know for sure that it's not all up to me. It is enough already.

I didn't know what would come next, but I knew it was enough already, and I could live in that.

One night in the fall of 2004, a few months after hearing about fear and hope, after hearing "enough already," and about a year and a half after that day of being *done* on a hillside in Papua New Guinea, Andy and I were having our nightly bubble bath.

We had become bubble bath experts by this time. When we started out, we could last about 20 minutes and then we'd be at the limits of our mutual capacities for vulnerability. But after 18 months, we had built some emotional muscle and we could be in there for a couple of hours sometimes, digging deep into thoughts and feelings, hearing each other out.

For some reason, that particular evening I remembered these words of Henri Nouwen from *Turn My Mourning Into Dancing*:

"The mystery of the dance is that its movements are discovered in the mourning. To heal is to let the Holy Spirit call me to dance, to believe again, even amid my pain, that God will orchestrate and guide my life.

"We tend, however, to divide our past into good things to remember with gratitude and painful things to accept or forget. This way of thinking, which at first seems quite natural, prevents us from allowing our whole past to be the source from which we live our future...

"Gratitude in its deepest sense means to live life as a gift to be received thankfully. And true gratitude embraces all of life: the good and the bad, the joyful and the painful, the holy and the not-so-holy. We do this because we become aware of God's life, God's presence in the middle of all that happens."

I first read those words back in Papua New Guinea, back in the deepest, darkest part of the pain, back when I had no idea what might lie ahead. I read those words and I thought, "This man is crazy! I can never be grateful for this! It will never happen!"

On the day of being *done*, I was so terrified, so overwhelmed, so lost. The pornography was so bad, and the situation was such a mess, and my kids were getting so hurt. I could not imagine how it could ever be okay again. It felt like a death blow.

But that night in the bubble bath, I caught a glimpse of the big picture. I realized that I was emotionally connected to Andy in a way I never dreamed possible. Andy was happier than he'd ever been. The kids were healing and growing and being amazing. I was enjoying relationships with other people that nurtured and sustained me. I was experiencing acceptance and personal freedom like I never had.

I saw all that, and I recalled those words of Henri Nouwen, and I started weeping. I said to Andy, "I'm grateful! I'm grateful!"

My vision for my life was control, but God had a dream for my wholeness and my freedom, and He would use anything and everything to make that dream a reality for me. And he wasn't just working for me, but for Andy and our kids, doing so much more than I could ever imagine. No mistake, no inadequacy, no sin could overcome God's work of redemption in our lives. God's presence was in the middle of every single thing.

It felt to me that terrible day on that hillside, as if I fell into the deepest, darkest, most trackless depths of the sea. Instead, that day, I was actually falling into Love, into grace, into healing.

As soon as I fell, He caught me.

Epilogue

Tawatana, Arosi New Testament Dedication Day, July 2005

"And the world cannot be discovered by a journey of miles, no matter how long, but only by a spiritual journey, a journey of one inch, very arduous and humbling and joyful, by which we arrive at the ground at our own feet, and learn to be at home." — Wendell Berry

In July 2005, the Arosi New Testament was finally done. Andy had worked on the final touches stateside, and it was at last typeset, printed, and shipped. A committee of Arosi people planned a dedication ceremony. The Bishop of Makira would attend, along with leaders of the Church of Melanesia and the South Seas Evangelical Church. Missionary friends of ours came from all over the Solomons, and from Australia. We flew out from the States, along with Andy's parents and my parents, to attend the dedication.

It would be our quickest trip ever to the village. We chartered a ship that would take all of us out to Tawatana, anchor overnight, and bring us all back to Honiara the next day, after the dedication. We arrived in Tawatana to find thousands of Arosi people gathered for the celebration, and a warm welcome waiting.

May, my self-appointed village mother, hadn't expected me to come to the dedication. She thought only Andy would be attending. When she saw me, we had a little re-enactment of that day at the beach, where she laughed and held me and called me her daughter.

Ben, Andy's original language teacher and our dear friend, had been diving on the reef for golden cowrie shells. He brought two of these beautiful, valuable shells over to our house that evening and presented them to our parents, saying thank you to them for allowing us to be in the Solomons all those years.

It seemed to me that we were having a dress rehearsal for the prophecy in Revelation:

After this I looked, and there before me was a great multitude that no one could count, from every nation, tribe, people and language, standing before the throne and before the Lamb. They were wearing white robes and were holding palm branches in their hands. (Revelation 7:9)

It was just like my neighbor Jean had told me, years before: "Even if we are separated here in this world, someday we'll all be together in heaven." For all of the differences between us, we had learned to love one another, and it was a love we would get to keep forever.

I thought, too, about the promise of the prophet Malachi:

And he shall purify the sons of Levi that they may offer unto the Lord an offering in righteousness. (Malachi 3:3)

I remembered how badly I had wanted to finish the project first, and take care of our own issues later. And I was so grateful that God knew better. I was so grateful that He had brought us to healing first, so that when we celebrated that dedication day, it was with clean hands and pure, joyful hearts.

Because of what Andy and I had been through together, and because of the healing God had done, the dedication was not just about publishing a book and presenting it to the community. The dedication, for us, was a celebration of love and relationship. It was about all of us loving each other, just as we are, all the way through. We are all His, all together, the precious Bride.

There was a church service, where the Arosi New Testament was read aloud, followed by an outdoor dedication service, where the Bishop admonished everyone to use the Arosi scriptures in their daily prayers. There was singing and dancing and speeches and feasting, lasting late into the night.

The next day, we boarded the ship again and had the usual experience of rough seas, barfing, and cockroach wars all the way back to Honiara. When we got off the ship, my mom said, "Honey, I'm so glad you don't have to do that anymore."

I said, "Me, too, Mom. Me too."

I'm grateful for so many things I don't have to do anymore.

I don't have to perform. I don't have to be perfect. I don't have to search for approval.

Everything I need is already here, in love.

There's the love I longed for, and thought I had to earn, that turned out to be mine all along.

There's the love that Andy and I found together, that shelters and nurtures and sustains our lives.

There's the love, so freely given, by so many people in so many places, that heals me every day.

All of that love, and infinitely more love than I can possibly imagine, is the Love of God that caught me and carries me and keeps me close, every step of the way.

About the Author

Kay Bruner grew up in Brazil, Nigeria, and the wilds of Kentucky. She and her husband, Andy, have raised their four children in the Solomon Islands, Papua New Guinea, and Texas. Kay has a BA in English, and an MA in Counseling. She is a Licensed Professional Counselor in private practice. She is the author of *Comfort Ye My People*, a daily Advent reader based on selections from Handel's *Messiah*. She blogs at www.kaybruner.com.

Credits

Images:
http://commons.wikimedia.org/wiki/File:MakiraMap.png
http://commons.wikimedia.org/wiki/File:Oceania-map_1-41000000.jpg
https://www.flickr.com/photos/efsavage/2314562874/

Sources:
Wendell Berry, *The Unforseen Wilderness*
William Bridges, *Transitions*
Frederick Buechner, *Beyond Words*
Soren Kierkegaard
Anne Lamott, *Traveling Mercies*
Anne Morrow Lindberg, *Gifts from the Sea*
Audre Lourde, *The Cancer Journals*
Brennan Manning, *Abba's Child*
Kathleen Norris, *The Cloister Walk*
Henri Nouwen, *The Inner Voice of Love*
Henri Nouwen, *Turn My Mourning Into Dancing*
Mark Twain

Made in the USA
Lexington, KY
19 September 2014